D1125858

GREEK ORACLES

Classical History and Literature

Editor

PROFESSOR H. T. WADE-GERY
F.B.A.
formerly *Wykeham Professor of Ancient History*
in the University of Oxford

GREEK ORACLES

H. W. Parke
Professor of Ancient History
Trinity College, Dublin

HUTCHINSON UNIVERSITY LIBRARY
LONDON

HUTCHINSON & CO (*Publishers*) LTD
178–202 Great Portland Street, London W1

London Melbourne Sydney
Auckland Bombay Toronto
Johannesburg New York

★

First published 1967

The vase on the cover of the paperback edition shows the purification of Orestes by Apollo at Delphi and is reproduced by courtesy of the Trustees of the British Museum

This book has been set in Fournier, printed in Great Britain on Smooth Wove paper by Anchor Press, and bound by Wm. Brendon, both of Tiptree, Essex

To H. T. Wade-Gery
who was the first to
teach me ancient history

CONTENTS

FOREWORD

An oracle for the present purpose is a formal statement from a god, usually given in answer to an enquiry, or else the place where such an enquiry could be made. The enquirer might be a state or a private individual, and the subject might vary widely, as also might the method by which the reply was elicited. But, however produced and for whatever purpose, oracles played a highly important part in the life of the ancient world at many periods.

To the Greeks the method of ascertaining the will of the gods was of particular importance because they possessed, generally speaking, no sacred books. Homer has sometimes been regarded by modern scholars as the bible of the ancient world. It was usual in antiquity to treat him as virtually infallible and his apparent errors or contradictions as problems to be explained away. Also, of course, Homer in a sense could be regarded as inspired. He invoked the muse at the beginning of each great epic and at other occasional points, and represented himself as guided by her knowledge of the facts. But in these respects Homer was not unique. Generally, his successors among the poets were also regarded as often taking on the functions of teachers. But in spite of this the Greeks and Romans did not use the works of Homer in the way in which Christians use their bible. When rhapsodes recited the poems at festivals they were not received like lessons read in a religious service, and private individuals, so far as we know, did not turn to their *Iliad* for spiritual guidance or comfort.

In Hellenistic and later periods, when the schools of philosophy had taken on to some extent the functions of religious sects, the works of some philosophers, such as Epicurus, were treated as inspired and used as canons of conduct and remedies against fear and anxiety. But they performed this service for a limited number of devoted individuals. To the Greek or Roman who sought the word of god on some particular issue the normal step would not be to consult a book but to enquire from a prophet.

Prophets could, of course, be of many kinds, from the individual with a reputation of being gifted in interpreting signs and omens to the holder of an official priesthood recognised by the state. For the purpose of the present discussion the individual, whether amateur or professional, is mostly excluded when we pass from Homer to the historic world. A comprehensive investigation of divination in its many forms would be too detailed for the present scale of treatment. But within the wide field of prophecy the oracular centre with its fixed location and its traditional methods of enquiry provides a particular manifestation of Greek religion and life.

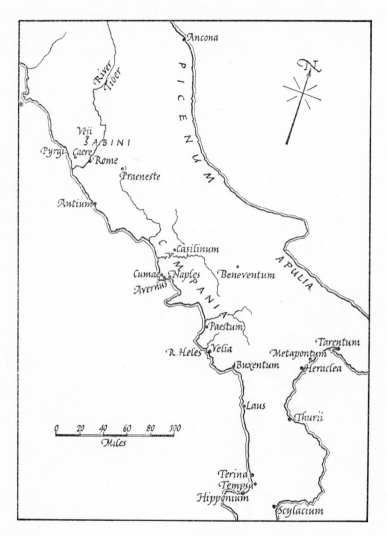

CLASSICAL ITALY

CLASSICAL GREECE AND ASIA MINOR

I

THE PROPHET AND THE
ORACLE IN HOMER

(I) PROPHETS

The prophet as the expounder of the will of god appears first in Homer, and there he usually is represented in a simple and primitive form. For instance, in the first book of the *Iliad,* when Achilles summons the Greeks together and asks why Apollo is angry as shown by the plague, he proposes that they should,

enquire of some prophet or sacrificial priest or even a dreamer of dreams, for a dream too comes from Zeus.

The answer to his question is supplied by the prophet Calchas, who is described as

the best of augurs [diviners by means of birds] who knew the present, that which was to come and that which had been before, and had led the ships of the Achaeans into Ilion by his gift of prophecy which Phoebus Apollo had given him.

Evidently Homer wished to characterise Calchas as an outstanding seer, but his powers are treated as a personal gift, and when he explains the reason for Apollo's anger he does not use any special technique to demonstrate the source of his information. To some extent his divination seems to be the result of an inborn intuition of the god's will. In so far as Homer indicates any method of procedure, the description 'the best of augurs' points to Calchas' use of the appearance and behaviour of birds as signs of divine purpose.[1]

[1] Superior figures refer to notes at end of each chapter.

The figure of Calchas taken in isolation might suggest that the prophet was ordinarily a professional in Homeric society. But other passages modify this view. The very same description 'the best of augers' (which may have been somewhat of a stock phrase in epic diction) is applied elsewhere to Helenus, the brother of Hector. At times he fights against the Greeks like any other Trojan hero, but also at other times he gives Hector sage advice and once is credited by Homer with having comprehended (apparently intuitively) the counsel of the gods.[2]

Apart from such intuitive knowledge of the gods, the observation of omens from such happenings as the behaviour of birds is a commonplace in both the *Iliad* and the *Odyssey*. These signs were not, like the Roman *auspicia*, looked for in a particular place after specific ritual, but were taken casually as observed. Also there was no need to seek a reputed prophet to provide an interpretation. When Telemachus is about to set out from Sparta on his return to Ithaca an eagle appears carrying off a goose. Pisistratus, Telemachus' companion, invites Menelaus to decide whether this is sent by god as a sign to the departing heroes or to their host. While Menelaus hesitates in thought, Helen offers that she will prophesy the future by interpreting the omen, and does so.[3]

So the picture which we get from Homer is that everyone took notice of unusual happenings of all sorts, but particularly the behaviour of birds, as possibly ominous, and that anyone might try to interpret their meaning, but some individuals were recognised as abnormally gifted in this accomplishment. The nearest that Homer comes to recognising prophets as a professional class is in the words which he puts into the mouth of Eumaeus, when Antinous taunts him with having introduced a strange beggar into the palace at Ithaca.

Who indeed would go himself and invite a stranger from elsewhere, unless it were one of those who do public work—a prophet or a healer of plagues or a carpenter or an inspired bard?[4]

This rather odd assemblage of professions is evidently determined by the idea that these were the typical specialists of Homeric society. While in that primitive world most men might be expected to turn their hand to any practical task that was needed by the household, there were a few functions in which it might be necessary to call in someone who in this particular line did not merely work for himself, but for the whole community, and might indeed have to be fetched as a stranger from outside.

So far the picture of prophets and prophetic methods derived from Homer is fairly consistent even if somewhat unsystematic in its working, and some scholars such as Martin P. Nilsson have maintained that Homer only knew 'inductive divination'—that is prophecy based on the observation of external signs. This statement ignores the implication that Calchas or Helenus could know the god's will intuitively, but still more it involves the disregard or misinterpretation of a passage in the *Odyssey* which clearly indicates a quite different kind of divination. The prophet concerned is Theoclymenus, an exile from blood-guilt, whom Telemachus accepts under his protection when returning from Pylos to Ithaca. He appears to have been invented by Homer as a character with two functions to fulfil. His original appeal to Telemachus gives an opportunity to show the young hero in a favourable light as already a mature and sympathetic man. Later at the climax, when the suitors are about to be faced with the contest of the bow, leading to their death at the hands of Odysseus, Theoclymenus provides a dramatic interlude—as a stranger accepted by Telemachus he was sitting in the palace amid the suitors, but his prophetic powers enable him to foresee the doom about to fall on them, and he both foretells it and flees in time. So as to satisfy his hearers about the credentials of this prophet whom he introduces into the narrative, Homer prefaces his first appearance with an elaborate genealogy tracing his descent from the legendary seer, Melampus, through a succession of diviners. It is the only place in the epic where prophecy appears to be a hereditary accomplishment. Also, his oracle when uttered takes on a unique form. On the principle that those whom they will destroy the gods first drive mad, Athena casts on the banqueting suitors an hysterical laughter ending in tears, and Theoclymemus cries out:

'Unhappy men, what is it that ails you? There is a shroud of night drawn over you from head to foot, a wailing bursts forth, and your cheeks are wet with tears. Blood drips from the walls and the roof-beams. The porch and the courtyard too are full of ghosts trooping down into the blackness of the pit. The sun has vanished from the sky and a cursed mist has spread over the earth.'

This powerful and dramatic passage is not sufficiently explained with Nilsson as 'poetic vision'. It is obviously 'second sight', whereby Theoclymenus passes from the spectacle of the hysterical suitors to see instead their destruction as later described by Homer. It is the one passage where the poet represents ecstatic prophecy—a state in which the seer is carried away from the world of the present to experience and describe a visionary revelation. It is perhaps significant that this episode which is unique in the epic is associated with a character who was probably invented for this particular occasion. Instead of reproducing part of the traditional formulae of the epic, Homer had branched out into something new.[5]

(2) ORACLE-CENTRES

So far we have only considered prophets and not oracle-centres in Homer, because only individual prophets appear directly in the *Iliad* and the *Odyssey*. The established centres of oracles are mentioned indeed, but only to a very limited extent and outside the main action. In the *Iliad*, Pytho, a primitive name for Delphi, appears in the 'Catalogue' and Achilles once refers vividly to,

all the treasures that the stone threshold of the archer keeps within, the threshold of Phoebus Apollo at rocky Pytho.

Presumably these treasures are the proceeds of the oracle, but Homer does not explain further. The only centre of prophecy specifically mentioned in the *Iliad* is Dodona. It is introduced at a great turning-point in the narrative. Achilles yielding to the appeals of Patroclus has agreed to send out the Myrmidons under his command against Hector. The occasion is marked by an elaborate description of Achilles' ceremony, leading up to a unique prayer to Zeus invoked under the title of Dodonaean:

'Lord Zeus, of Dodona, Pelasgian, dwelling afar, ruling over hard-wintered Dodona, and around dwell the Selli your interpreters of unwashen feet, sleeping on the ground.'[6]

The passage was not merely unique in the epic, but also by the time that Homeric commentators could work on it there was evidently no survival of the institution in this form on the site and no extant mention in other literature which could elucidate its problems. If taken as it stands, the passage indicates that Homer thought it plausible for a special occasion to make Achilles pray, not to a god dwelling in his own Thessalian kingdom, but across the range of Pindus in what was later Epirus. There the worship of Zeus was ministered by people called the Selli, who observed curious customs of abstaining from washing and sleeping on the ground. It is possible, as some modern scholars prefer, to treat these features as traces of primitive barbarism of no religious significance. But in the context it is more reasonable to suppose that they had a ritual purpose. If the Selli were members of a culture already highly advanced in civilisation, it is perhaps unlikely that their ritual would have taken this backward form. The best explanation is that they were members of a primitive tribe who retained as a result of their religious taboos certain vestiges of barbarism.

That their religion was concerned with an oracle is only indicated by the one word 'interpreters'. Ancient commentators took it in this sense, but noted that Homer did not use the normal word for prophet implying by derivation 'one who speaks on behalf of a god', but instead this term which indicates 'one who suggests a meaning'. The special appropriateness of this description emerges if we consider the mention in the *Odyssey* of the same oracle. It occurs in a much more matter-of-fact context than the highly emotional prayer of Achilles. On two parallel occasions Odysseus in disguise is wishing to convey the suggestion that his return to Ithaca is imminent. So he alleges that he has heard news of the wanderer on the mainland in Thesprotia.

'He has gone,' they said, 'to Dodona to listen to the counsel of Zeus from his high-foliaged oak, how he should return to the rich land of Ithaca, now that he had been absent long: whether to return openly or secretly.'[7]

Here for the first time we encounter what we do not find in the *Iliad*, a description of an enquiry at an oracle. It is not authentic, but a fiction invented by Odysseus. At the same time Homer no doubt intended the story to seem plausible when put into the mouth of his character. The passage fits well with the brief allusion in the *Iliad*. For if the responses of Zeus at Dodona were in some way extracted from his oak-tree, there would be need of ritually qualified interpreters to convey their meaning to the enquirer. Also the prophet as seen elsewhere in Homer was most typically one who could expound the hidden meaning of the phenomena of nature. The Selli and the oak-tree would be regarded in one way as a particular example of this practice.

Before we consider Dodona further, we should, however, examine the one reference to the Delphic oracle in the *Odyssey*. This occurs in one of the epic recitations put into the mouth of the bard Demodocus at the court of Alcinous. He sang of

'the strife between Odysseus and Achilles, how once they quarrelled in the rich banquet with outrageous words and Agamemnon, lord of heroes, rejoiced at heart, because the best of the Achaeans were quarrelling. For thus Phoebus Apollo had spoken to him in prophecy in holy Pytho when he crossed the stone threshold to consult the oracle. For then indeed a beginning of woe was rolling to the Trojans and Greeks through the counsels of Zeus.'[8]

This incident which Demodocus related (unlike the other lays attributed to him) is not recorded elsewhere in Greek tradition. Evidently one is to suppose that before sailing against Troy Agamemnon had consulted Apollo and had received an oracle which foretold as a sign of success a quarrel between the best of the Greeks. Agamemnon is represented as seeing the fulfilment of this prophecy in an otherwise unrecorded dispute between Odysseus and Achilles. The *Iliad* shows no knowledge of this story: its famous dispute is between Achilles and Agamemnon himself. But that famous quarrel in which Agamemnon was himself a party would not have satisfied the oracle. Though the fulfilment of the prophecy is not explained in this passage, it could most convincingly have been found in the dispute between Ajax and Odysseus over the armour of Achilles, which in the Epic Cycle immediately preceded the chain of events which brought about the capture of Troy. The dispute over the armour is an episode already known to the author of the *Odyssey* and no doubt he expected the allusion to be recognised by his hearers.

From our present point of view the interest of the passage lies to a large extent in its contrast with the previously discussed description of a consultation at Dodona. There the oak of Zeus was the source of the prophecy; here Apollo himself—which would be equally valid if the oracle came from a Pythia speaking by inspiration in his name. Again the enquiry at Dodona is so framed as to ask for a reply in a single word deciding between the alternatives offered. Odysseus wanted to know whether he should return openly or secretly, and the response need only indicate the god's approval of one or other course.

Agamemnon presumably asked about the success of his intended expedition. But the reply does not seem to have been designed to distin-
guish between alternative results. It apparently was in a discursive
verbal form and offered him the prospect of success, but only in rather
unlikely circumstances—when the best of the Greeks had first
quarrelled.

Thus, though the Pythia is not mentioned, this passage in the
Odyssey conforms to the usual features of later traditional stories about
consultations of the Delphic oracle. The leader of an expedition asks
for success and is promised it in ambiguous phrases which, though
ultimately fulfilled, lead first to misunderstanding and disappointment.

So in the matter of oracle-centres as in the subject of individual
prophets the Homeric Epic in different passages illustrates quite
different methods in operation. The allusions to Dodona fit with the
divination by means of natural signs which is usual in Homer. The
description of a Delphic consultation is parallel to the picturesquely
symbolic wording and ecstatic prophecy of Theoclymenus. As with
the differences between the Homeric descriptions of arms and armour,
which at one time fit an early Mycenaean period and at another suggest
the Archaic Greek, so in matters of religious institutions we may feel
that Homer is at one time drawing on highly traditional material
from the distant past and at another using contemporary practice as
his model. In this way it would be impossible on the basis of the Epic
alone to trace the beginnings of the Greek oracles, but by calling in
archaeology some further progress at least can be made in establishing
the probable pattern of development.

NOTES

1. Achilles' question: Homer, *Il.* *1*, 62; Calchas: *Il.* *1*, 69
2. 'Best of Augurs': *Il.* *1*, 69 (Calchas), *6*, 76 (Helenus); Helenus giving advice: *7*.
   44; fighting: *12*, 94 and *13*, 576
3. *Od.* *15*, 160
4. *Od.* *17*, 382
5. *Od.* *20*, 351, on which contrast W. B. Stanford's commentary and M. P,
   Nilsson, *Geschichte der griechischen Religion*, 1^2, 166
6. Pytho: *Il.* *2*, 519 and *9*, 405; Dodona: *Il.* *2*, 750 and *16*, 234
7. *Od.* *14*, 327 and *19*, 296
8. *Od.* *8*, 79

2

PRIMITIVE DODONA

Dodona is situated near the foot of a low hill which lies towards the head of the deep valley of Tcharacovista, some twelve miles from Jannina in north-west Greece. The sanctuary is at a height of 1600 feet above sea level, and to the west of it Mount Tomaros towers over the view. The region was earlier well wooded and still is freely scattered with deciduous trees. The bottom of the valley is marshy in places and Mount Tomaros produces plentiful springs. The site was dug extensively by C. Carapanos in 1875–6 in what was less an archaeological excavation than a search for antiquities. It is chiefly due to the intermittent but persistent work of D. Evangelides between 1929 and 1958 in exploring the sanctuary that it has been possible for S. I. Dakaris to produce a picture of the various stages by which it developed.[1]

If we go back to the period of the Trojan war, Dodona was extensively inhabited by a primitive people who used a handmade pottery of Neolithic style. They appear to have had no permanent dwellings, but probably were a pastoral community coming to these well-watered uplands each summer and living in temporary huts. Their periodic visits left a thick layer of broken pottery on the site. There is no certain evidence from archaeology for religious worship, but obviously it would be quite consistent with the primitive settlement which it shows to suppose that it centred on an oak-tree which was regarded as sacred to the god who thundered from heaven.

So far all the results of excavation suggest that in the second millennium B.C. there was no occupation of Dodona by the people of central

Greece and the Peloponnese and even that intercourse with those parts was at most very sporadic. No Helladic or Mycenaean pottery has been found on the site. Finds of Late Helladic III sherds and a tholos tomb on the coast of Epirus suggest that the Mycenaeans towards the end of their civilisation may have penetrated the Adriatic coastal regions, but not farther inland. Only two swords found at Dodona, one a bronze rapier, the other an iron broad-sword, suggest that either occasionally weapons had travelled by trade to the far north-west or even perhaps that a warrior or two from Mycenaean Greece had penetrated as far as Dodona and left a dedication to the god of battles.

This lack of influence from the Mediterranean centres of culture both fits the primitive pottery of the neighbourhood and also is quite consistent with its religious practices. Nowhere else in Greece in classical times do we hear of Zeus as worshipped at a special sacred oak. The tree as a species was associated with him in Homer just as the laurel is associated with Apollo, but unlike the laurel the oak plays scarcely any part in his rites of worship. Trees appear to have been important in Minoan religion, judging by the representations on gems of what appear to be religious ceremonies. But the affinities of these practices are with the tree and vegetation cults of the Near East.[2] The oak of Dodona has its nearest analogies not in Greece so much as in Italy and still more in such distant parts of northern Europe as pagan Prussia, where the Indo-European sky-god was worshipped locally at a sacred oak. Also it is in Italy and again still more in Prussia that there can be found analogies for the curious cult practices which Homer attributed to the Selli. As we have said, their customs of not washing their feet and sleeping on the ground had evidently died out by the time that the Homeric commentators got to work on the passage. Also no analogies were found in Classical Greece. But the Flamen Dialis in Rome had to sleep on a special bed whose feet were smeared with a thin layer of mud, and Frazer has plausibly explained this as 'a mitigation of an older custom of sleeping on the ground'.[3] Also, in Prussia the priest of the god Potrimpo was bound to sleep for three nights on the bare earth before he sacrificed to the deity. Abstention from washing the feet appears to have no analogies in northern Europe, but one of those who tried to explain the Homeric passage, Alexander of Pleuron, a Hellenistic scholar, appears to have heard of the taboo in Italy, for he mentions it in connection with a theory that the Selli were descended from the Tyrrhenians and had retained this ancestral custom from their origin. Alternatively, the nearest analogies are to be found in India where the Vedas contain instruction about avoiding washing as a ritual practice and where also in the Agnihotris, the Brahmanical fire-priests, Frazer can find another instance of the rule of sleeping on the ground.[4]

These Italian, northern European and Indian parallels to the practices of Dodona are not in any instance especially associated with prophecy rather than with general worship of a male god. Their resemblance is best explained by the supposition that they are essentially primitive in character and spring from roots which are shared by the rudimentary cults of these different regions to which the Indo-European peoples spread. No theological explanation is offered by our Greek sources, and perhaps by the time they first came to Dodona the Selli were already observing these traditional rules without understanding their original purpose. But the simplest explanation would be to suppose that the priests of Zeus had originally been regarded as beings of a special potency. They had acquired this by contact with the earth and must not wipe it off by washing their feet or sleeping on a bed instead of resting on the bare earth itself. To those who saw the chief manifestation of the god in a massive tree the feeling that man himself, like the tree, drew strength from the ground in its neighbourhood would be a natural and reasonable belief.

We need not suppose, as some scholars have done, that the practice points to the previous existence of a cult of mother earth at Dodona. There is no evidence apart from these taboos to suggest that Zeus was preceded by a female deity, as was probably true at Olympia. In classical times in Epirus Zeus had a consort Dione, but everything suggests that she had never existed independently of him. Also, as we have seen, the Indo-European analogies are never connected with any indications that the male god had stepped into the place of a female predecessor.

Similarly also there is no need to suppose that 'sleeping on the ground' points to the use of incubation as a means of divination. We shall have occasion to notice elsewhere in Greece the practice whereby an enquirer might be made to sleep in a sanctuary so as to receive direct from the god or goddess the revelation which he needed. But in all such instances the deity consulted was not the sky-god Zeus, but a mother goddess of the earth or a hero with similar associations. Also it was not the prophet who slept on the ground, but the enquirer, and the prophet's function was simply to supervise the appropriate accompaniment of ritual and interpret the dream when the enquirer had described it.

At Dodona, instead, as we have seen, the oak-tree was the manifestation of the god and the vehicle of his prophecy. The Selli were his interpreters. That the tree in some sense 'spoke' is implied not only by the *Odyssey*, but also by an equally ancient legend. In the story of the Argonauts their ship the Argo was gifted with the power of speech and traditionally exercised it on three occasions at least: when first launched, when its original helmsman died and a new one had to be chosen, and when it had reached the furthest and most perilous part of its voyage. These episodes no doubt formed part of the basic legend of the first ship to sail the seas—a story old enough to be referred to in the *Odyssey* as familiar to all. It is significant, then, that the origin of the Argo's power of speech was put down to the fact that Athena had taken a timber from the oak-tree of Dodona and fitted it in the keel. Evidently the idea behind the legend was that since the oak of Dodona could talk, so also timber derived from it could employ this miraculous gift wherever it was placed.[5]

It is highly appropriate to find this legendary motive in the *Argonautica*. For evidently in its earliest forms this was a story of Thessaly, connected with the heroic kings of that region and with the ship itself setting out from Iolcos. We have seen how in the *Iliad* the prayer to Zeus of Dodona is put into the mouth of Achilles, whose father was a famous Argonaut and whose kingdom lay in northern Greece. Again, significantly, the only other reference to Dodona in the *Iliad* is as a place-name in a kingdom attached as a sort of vague annex to Thessaly. Whether this correctly illustrated the political relations of Dodona at the time of the Trojan war, there is little doubt that it rightly suggests that it was a distant and little-known region connected with the rest of Greece only by the Metsovo pass through the Pindus range—though no doubt it was already recognised as a source of oracles given by a talking oak. After the shifts of population during the Dark Ages its link with Thessaly seems to have broken, and later, as we shall see, Thessaly looked south through Thermopylae to Delphi for its prophecies: not over the Pindus to Dodona.

One other primitive feature can probably be connected with Dodona in its earliest periods: this is a talking dove. The evidence for it is not so clear as for the oak. Homer does not mention it, but it may be more than a mere coincidence that in the same passage in the *Odyssey* where he refers to the Argo he also mentions doves as specially associated with Zeus.[6] In classical times the eagle had become exclusively the bird of the king of the gods, but Homer shows that this was not always so in the further past, though, once more, the Homeric commentators found it difficult to cite parallels. So far as Dodona is concerned the dove appears in the various forms of the foundation legend of the oracle. These are only extant from late sources, but evidently went back to much more primitive origins. In various versions the bird seated on the oak warns a wood-cutter who is about to chop down the tree that it is sacred to Zeus and prophetic. It may seem an unnecessary superfluity for a dove to speak from the branches of the oak if the tree could talk itself, but folklore abounds in such incongruities. Later traditions, as we shall see, represented the doves themselves as speaking oracles, but sometimes for this purpose they were said not to be birds, but priestesses called doves. However, it is sufficient to suppose that in the second millennium B.C. the Selli, the observers of strange taboos, living in a wild and distant land, if consulted by enquirers sought the oracles of Zeus from a sacred oak at Dodona in whose branches nested doves which also were sacred to the god. How precisely the oak or the doves were consulted we are not told. The practice in this form was dead by classical times. So we cannot be sure whether the prophets had to wait until, with the help of the breeze, the oak-tree groaned or its branches rustled. Dodona was a windy spot—so the signs may have been frequently available. Alternatively perhaps the calls of the ring-doves, one of the more loquacious of the larger birds, could be taken as speech. Greek legend knew elsewhere of prophets who could understand the talk of birds. One of them, Mopsus, was traditionally connected with Dodona, and was an Argonaut.

If so, we can suppose that what to the ordinary individual listening as an enquirer were the creaks and rustles of a great tree and the calls of birds, could be interpreted by the Selli as the words of Zeus. We have no genuine early evidence to show whether these words were really composed by the Selli into a discursive statement or whether perhaps as the *Odyssey* seems to suggest the question which Zeus was asked to answer was a simple alternative, and all the Selli needed to say was that the god had shown his approval of one proposition and rejection of the other. Anyway such rudimentary divination by natural manifestations which needed to be interpreted by a prophet is quite consistent with the more primitive stages illustrated by episodes in the Greek epic which we have already considered, and it is this evidence, literary and archaeological, which confirms the claim which Dodona made in later times that it was the oldest of Greek oracles.

NOTES

1. For a fuller discussion and citation of sources: see H. W. Parke, *Oracles of Zeus*, ch. 6
2. See Parke, *Oracles of Zeus*, ch. 2
3. Aulus Gellius, 10, 15, 14. Sir James Frazer *Golden Bough*, 11^3, 248, where also the pagan Prussians are discussed
4. Alexander of Pleuron: Scholia A., *Il.* 16, 235. The Agnihotris: Frazer, *Golden Bough*, loc. cit
5. The oak and the Argonauts: see Parke, *Oracles of Zeus*, 13 ff.
6. For Dodona and the dove: see Parke, *Oracles of Zeus*, 34 ff.

3

THE CAVERN AND THE APOLLINE MEDIUM

(1) THE CAVERN

Homer, as we have seen, recognises Dodona and Delphi as oracles, but names none in the Peloponnese or Crete. Yet it is obviously improbable that these regions had no sources of prophecy or methods of formal divination in early times. Actually evidence for consultation of the gods at special localities and by a specific method can be vaguely surmised on the basis of some scattered literary evidence. This combines to suggest that in primitive times the deities could be approached by entering caves. The best attested example was the sanctuary of Ge, the earth-goddess, near Aegeira in Achaea. There the priestess after she had been chosen had to abstain from sexual intercourse thenceforth and must have previously had only one husband. Her purity was tested by an ordeal of drinking bulls' blood which was supposed to be fatal to the unchaste. When properly tested the priestess entered a cavern and returned inspired with prophecy. The evidence for this ritual comes from comparatively late sources such as Pliny the Elder and Pausanias—but Pausanias, a connoisseur in these matters, believed the cult-statue of Ge at Aegeira to be among the oldest wooden figures, and it would not be surprising to find that a very primitive custom had survived in this out-of-the-way neighbourhood.[1]

For traces of other such associations of a cavern, the earth-goddess and prophecy we may note Olympia when Zeus appears to have been preceded by Ge who traditionally had had an oracle there. Also in classical times, when the oracle of earth had been superseded by that of Zeus, there was still a place called the Stomion—the cavern-mouth, with an altar to Themis who in Delphic theology was the prophetic daughter of Ge. This sounds to be a rather sophisticated *mise-en-scène*, such as would probably be produced in the fourth century B.C. or later when Olympia was very much associated with Delphi. But it need not be therefore rejected as evidence that once there had been a cavern or hollow in the ground at Olympia which was entered by the earth-goddess's priestess when seeking prophecy. If so, this must have corresponded to the tradition at Delphi that there had been a cult of Ge before the coming of Apollo, and to the recurrent references to a chasm or a cave connected with the oracle.[2]

Neither at Olympia nor at Delphi has excavation been able to find the cave. But elsewhere, particularly in Crete, there is abundant indication that caves were the scene of primitive worship. The best example, perhaps, is the cavern of Eleithyia at Amnisos. It has the distinction of being mentioned in the *Odyssey*, and when explored by Marinatos in 1929 proved to contain pottery in unbroken sequence from the Neolithic to early Christian times.[3] Of course such finds do not prove the use of the cave for oracular purposes as distinct from general worship. But also, if the cavern was entered to make offerings to the gods, it would be natural to use the occasion to try to ascertain their will. Indeed the very effect of entering a cave tends to be eerie and potentially numinous. Where this place was associated with traditions of power and sanctity it would not be surprising if the priestess who had been underground and emerged again to the light of day appeared dazed and beside herself. To the ancient world this was not a psychological phenomenon of dissociation, but the manifestation of the power of the divine.

Hence it is no wonder that the association of the entering of caves and prophecy crops up in various other directions in the Greek world as well as at sanctuaries of the earth-goddess. It is a feature, as we shall see, of sibyls and their shrines, and also the oracle of Trophonius at Lebadeia had a very peculiar and special use of a cavern, while late temples such as that of Apollo at Claros had underground structures devoted to the purposes of divination.

(2) THE APOLLINE MEDIUM

So far there has been no occasion to discuss the god whom the Greeks of classical times associated most with prophecy. This was Apollo, who has often been regarded as the most truly Hellenic of the Greek gods. Yet it is fairly clear that he was not originally among the deities worshipped by the Greeks when they first settled in Hellas. He appears to have come in as an intruder during the Dark Ages between the Mycenaean and the Archaic Greek periods. This supposition fits with the Greek traditions which represent him, for instance, as arriving at Delphi and finding it already occupied. Also the belief that he was not worshipped by the Mycenaeans is confirmed by the fact that so far at least his name has not been deciphered in any Linear B tablets, though even Dionysus, often regarded as a late-comer to the Greek pantheon, appears to be named there.

So far most scholars would be in agreement, but there has at least in earlier years been much argument over the question from what direction Apollo came.[4] In the late nineteenth century it was probably more usual to suppose that he came from the north. This theory seemed to harmonise with the wonderful picture in the Homeric *Hymn to Apollo* of the young god passing through Thessaly, Euboea and Boeotia until at last he finds the home for his oracle at Delphi. But clearly the poet's description is based imaginatively on the idea that Apollo came from Olympus in the literal sense of the mountain in northern Greece. Also the cult practice connecting Apollo with the Vale of Tempe and the procession from there to Delphi every ninth year need not be interpreted as enacting the direction of Apollo's coming. The association of him with the Hyperboreans, the mysterious and blessed race who live beyond the north wind, is better evidence for a possible northern origin. In classical times at Delphi it was believed that Apollo absented himself for three months in the depth of winter to reside with the Hyperboreans. But these legendary folk must not be taken as giving a clear geographical direction for Apollo's origin. They evidently were a folktale creation originally and dwelt in a place that never existed, 'east of the sun and west of the moon'.

A northern origin of Apollo has been more often accepted, as one may surmise, because it seemed to fit romantically with the character of the god. He was, as we have said, often regarded in modern times

as the most Hellenic of the gods and with that view went the feeling
that he represented a Nordic strain in opposition to the darker side of
the Mediterranean deities. Again the opposition of the Apolline and
the Dionysiac, known to the ancient world, but made popular in
modern times by Nietzche, was best interpreted if a pure Apollo from
the north were opposed to an orgiastic Dionysus from the east.

Yet on the whole the balance of evidence seems to point to the east
as being his true place of origin. For oriental connections we may note
that exceptionally among Greek gods he was particularly associated
with the seventh day of the month, traditionally his birthday. The
Greek lunar calendar was based on the number ten, while the seven-day
week is oriental. Again the one non-Hellenic country with which he
was strongly associated by tradition was Lycia, in south-west Asia
Minor. He himself was called Lyceius, and the name of his mother,
Leto, appears to be derived directly from the Lycian word for woman
'lada'. Also it is remarkable how he is treated in the *Iliad*. While some
of the gods favour the Greeks and others the Trojans, Apollo is the
most consistent and conspicuous enemy of the Greek side. The poem
starts with the grim picture of the god shooting with his avenging
arrows in punishment for the insult to his priest, and the final words
of the dying Hector are to foretell to Achilles how he will perish
through the help of Phoebus. Of course, Apollo must long have been
accepted by the Greeks and have been given temples and worship
before Homer wrote. But the feeling seems still to have persisted to
his day that Apollo was the deity most naturally to be viewed as the
protector of people in Asia Minor.

Wherever he appeared Apollo was associated with prophecy. This
is true even in Lycia, his non-Hellenic home. There his most famous
shrine was at Patara, where according to Herodotus a peculiar ritual
was observed.

The woman who is the mouthpiece of the god whenever it takes place
(for the oracle is not there at all times) then is shut in with the god by night
within the temple.[5]

Herodotus cites this practice as an analogy for the similar arrangement
for a consort of the god at Babylon and at Egyptian Thebes, where the
deities were Bel and Amon-Ra. The very fact that Herodotus has to
quote Lycia as furnishing the nearest example is because this was not

a normal practice in Greek religion and is never found in temples of Apollo in Greek lands. Here it is worth noting to show how, though the god of Lycia may have had a common name and to some extent a common origin with the Apollo of the Hellenes, his ritual practices were different and linked him more closely with the Orient. Evidently it was part at least of the mechanism of the oracle at Patara that the prophetess, who spoke in the god's name, was believed to derive her inspiration to some extent at least by sleeping with him in his temple. The fact, noted by Herodotus, that she did not sleep there when the oracle was not functioning proves the causal connection with prophecy.

Curiously enough, as though in direct contradiction of this Lycian belief, the Greeks told an opposite legend about Cassandra. She had won the love of Apollo and asked as the price of her favours the gift of prophecy. This the god bestowed, but then she refused her side of the compact, and Apollo avenged himself by the curse that her prophecies, though true, would never be believed. This legend is not indicated at any point in the *Iliad* or the *Odyssey*, though Cassandra as a daughter of Priam finds a place in both epics. So presumably the story is post-Homeric. But in his *Agamemnon* Aeschylus introduces it as though familiar to his audience.[6] The prevalence of the story shows that to the Greeks the gift of prophecy in a woman was associated with the idea of virginity and not with the position of consort to a god.

Actually so far as our evidence goes for archaic periods the normal mouthpiece of Apollo in Greek temples was not a woman, but a man. This is a fact which scholars seem unwilling to accept, but the evidence, though limited, is reasonably clear. Of the Asiatic sanctuaries there is no evidence one way or the other for Branchidae in the archaic period. When it was revived in the Hellenistic age after an interruption of a century and a half a woman acted as mouthpiece, but the restoration at this time was obviously influenced by Delphi and so is no proof of the primitive practice. In Claros, on the other hand, whose oracular activity never was interrupted so far as is known, the spokesman in later times was a male prophet as is clearly stated in our literary sources and confirmed by the local inscriptional records. On the Greek mainland the one archaic example is from the sanctuary of Apollo Ptoios in Boeotia, and for it we have the virtually contemporary record of

Herodotus. He describes it as one of the episodes in a series of consultations of Boeotian oracles made in 480–79 B.C. by Mys, a Lycian, as an agent of the Persian general, Mardonius. The god's mouthpiece astounded the local officials by addressing the Asiatic enquirer in a barbarian language which he recognised as Carian. The speaker is referred to in Herodotus' narrative, and in the later authorities derived from him, as a man, and the context shows clearly that he was supposed to have spoken directly under the inspiration of Apollo.[7] This last point is worth emphasising, because at Delphi though the god's mouthpiece was a woman—the *Pythia*—the oracle was officially conveyed to the enquirers by a man, the *Prophetes*. But evidently at Claros and at the Ptoion sanctuary Apollo's inspiration came directly to a male spokesman, and it is much more plausible that this had been the usual procedure in early times at temples of Apollo in Greek lands. Apart from the revived oracle of Branchidae in the Hellenistic period the only other example where a woman appears as the mouthpiece of Apollo, apart from Delphi, is the sanctuary of Apollo Pythaeus at Argos. There our evidence comes from Pausanias in late times and is combined with a claim that the oracle was founded from Delphi.[8] So though a ritual which Pausanias describes is not Pythian, it is reasonable to suppose that the sex of the prophetess as the chosen mouthpiece of the god was influenced by imitation of Delphi.

If, then, we accept the view that Apollo as a god of prophecy was introduced to the Greeks by the Anatolians during the Dark Ages, it is to be taken that from whatever precise direction he came—whether from Lycia or from some common archetypal source—he was not accepted by the Greeks as a god whose mouthpiece was his female consort. His spokesman usually was a man; which both seems more what one might expect and corresponds to the general Hellenic practice, by which gods are served by male priests and goddesses by priestesses. One feature, however, seems to be common to the two examples of male priests which we have quoted, and also to the Pythia. The prophet at Claros spoke in verse and evidently was popularly supposed at least to use this medium as a result of direct inspiration. The prophet of Apollo Ptoios on one occasion spoke in Carian, and, while this was a very exceptional manifestation, the explanation accepted evidently was that Apollo had inspired him directly with this strange tongue. Similarly, the Pythia was the direct mouthpiece of

Apollo, inspired by him, and when she used the first-person singular she was not meaning to refer to herself, but to the god.

The particular factors at work in producing the ritual of the Delphic oracle can be discussed more fully later, but first it is worth while to note how generally Apolline sanctuaries have some evidence to show that they were oracle centres. In the Classical period the great fame of Delphi tended to overshadow all the other oracles, but both in the archaic period, so far as our evidence goes, and again in the Hellenistic period when the influence of Delphi was reduced and localised, other oracles of Apollo existed and even flourished. One group is scattered along the seaboard of Asia Minor from Branchidae in Caria to Thymbra in the Troad; of the islands Lesbos and Chios had Apolline oracles, and Delos, though later mainly famous as his birthplace, evidently once had been a centre of divination. On the Greek mainland the main group is in Boeotia, with one outlying example in Thessaly and another at Argos in the Peloponnese. Delphi is the most westerly point of his advance, and we do not know whether he came there from Boeotia on the route described in the earlier part of the *Homeric Hymn to Apollo* or instead brought his worshippers by sea from Crete as narrated in the last section of the same hymn.

NOTES

1. Aegeira: Pliny, *Historia Naturalis*, 28, 147 and Pausanias 7, 25, 13
2. Olympia: Pausanias, *5*, 14, 10. For Delphi: see H. W. Parke and D. E. W. Wormell, *Delphic Oracle*, *1*, 11 and 19 ff.
3. Hom., *Od. 19*, 188 and S. Marinatos, *Crete and Mycanae* (1960), plate 1 and p. 115
4. For Apollo and the Hyperboreans: see M. P. Nilsson, *Geschichte der griechischen Religion*, *1²*, 548, and for his eastern connections, id., 559
5. Herodotus, *1*, 182
6. Aeschylus, *Agamemnon*, 1202 ff.
7. Claros: cf. infra, p. 137; Apollo Ptoios: Hdt. *8*, 135
8. Pausanias, *2*, 24, 1

4

PRIMITIVE DELPHI

Archaeological excavation has shown that there had been a rather poor and thinly inhabited village scattered over the site from near Castalia to the later temple of Apollo.[1] It appears to date at earliest from Late Helladic III (1400 B.C.), and no structure which could be classed as a sanctuary has been found. The few small clay images excavated might well belong to private cults. But the one startling exception is a marble rhyton (sacred pouring vessel) in the shape of a lioness's head which is clearly Minoan in origin. It seems to be not only earlier than anything else there, but also to belong to a quite different culture from that otherwise shown by the finds. Probably it was brought in from elsewhere and was already old when it reached Delphi. It points to contact with Minoan cult practices, but the contact may have been so distant and indirect that no conclusion about the worship at Delphi in Late Helladic III can safely be drawn from it.

There is more evidence from another part at Delphi, namely the site of the classical shrine of Athena Pronaia on the east of Castalia. There, as excavation has shown, there was not a settlement, but a cult centre going back to Mycenaean times. The predecessor of Athena was evidently also herself a goddess. In fact if we accept the view that the literary evidence points to an earth-goddess as the previous occupant of Delphi before Apollo, it will be more likely that her sanctuary was in this neighbourhood than where the classical temple of the god was built.

B

The Mycenaean village may have been destroyed at the beginning of the Dark Ages. Traces of burning were found at the appropriate level. Anyway there was no continuous and uninterrupted development, but rather a fresh start in the early eighth century. From the closing stages of the geometric period objects intended as dedications are found in increasing numbers on the site of Apollo's sanctuary, so that evidently the cult may have arrived somewhat earlier in the Dark Ages, but began to flower with the period of Greek colonisation.

It is interesting archaeologically that a number of important finds from the earlier archaic periods show clear affinities or actual derivation from Crete. For, as we have mentioned, the *Homeric Hymn to Apollo* ends by describing how,

Phoebus Apollo then took it in mind whom he would bring of men as his worshippers who would serve him in rocky Pytho. Then while pondering he was aware of a swift ship on the wine-dark sea, and in it were good men and many—Cretans from Minoan Knosos who offer sacrifices to the lord Apollo and announce the oracles of Phoebus Apollo of the golden sword whatever he speaks in prophecy from the laurel-tree beneath the gorges of Parnassus.[2]

The *Hymn* gives a picturesque description how the god in the form of a large dolphin directed the ship on a new course, not to Pylos, its original objective, but to the harbour of Crisa. There he appeared in human shape and led them to his temple at Delphi and commissioned them to be his priests. Some scholars have seen in the evident archaeological links between early archaic Delphi and Crete a basis of fact behind this façade of legend, and it is possible that the cult of Apollo was introduced by sea from Crete rather than overland from Boeotia. Apollo was a favourite god of the Dorians in Crete. It could be objected that while in Boeotia Apollo had several well-known centres of prophecy, he is never shown by our evidence to have had oracles in Crete. But in the very defective state of our literary evidence for Crete in early times this may be an unsound deduction.

If Apollo came to Delphi as a god of prophecy towards the end of the Dark Ages, what technique did he bring with him and what, if any, did he find there before him? The *Homeric Hymn*, from which we have already quoted, contains an earlier section describing how, 'far-darting Apollo, you first went through the earth seeking an oracle-centre for men'.[3] The god, as we have seen, descends from Olympus and, coming through Boeotia, finds the place 'at Crisa under snowy Parnassus'. First Apollo lays out his temple and then at a neighbouring spring he slays a formidable she-serpent. The killing of the snake is treated as the removal of a local nuisance. Evidently the story is based to some extent on the folk motive of St George and the Dragon and many other heroes slaying monsters. Some scholars have been content to leave it at that: the dragon is just a monster with a significance symbolic of the forces of evil.[4]

Yet later Delphic theology represented Apollo as preceded at the sanctuary by the earth-goddess as a source of prophecy. In the *Eumenides* of Aeschylus the prologue is spoken by the Pythia who begins with a prayer of invocation.

'First in this prayer I honour before the other gods Earth, the primal prophetess. After her Themis, who was the second to sit here in her mother's oracle, as a tradition says. In the third place, willingly and not perforce, after her sat another child of Earth, the Titaness, Phoebe. She gave it as a birthday gift to Phoebus who takes his name from her.'

Then, with obvious appeal to Athenian patriotism, Aeschylus puts into her mouth a description how Apollo came from Delos to Attica, and thence with an escort of Athenians to Delphi. There is no reference to the she-dragon: only a vague allusion to the Athenians pacifying the savage land: the purpose is evidently to suggest that there had been no conflict between Apollo and a previous occupant. It is nearly half a century later in a chorus from Euripides' *Iphigenia in Tauris* when we first encounter explicitly a combination of these two opposite traditions.[5] There Apollo is described as slaying 'a serpent, a huge monster of Earth who ministered the oracle of the earth-goddess'. When by occupying the prophetic tripod at Delphi, Apollo had driven Themis, the daughter of Earth, from the place, Earth revenged herself by sending in the night prophetic dreams to men. This competition against Apollo's oracle was threatening to deprive him of his glory as prophet. But he appealed to Zeus who stopped Earth's dream oracles and restored the pre-eminence to Apollo.

This version of the myth presented by Euripides is evidently highly sophisticated, but it need not therefore be discounted in the essential point which it makes: that the dragon (who for Euripides and thereafter is male) was a representative of the earth-goddess and that

Apollo's conquest of the dragon is a forceable acquisition of an oracular centre.

The appropriateness of a snake being associated with the earth-goddess is obvious and suits with the indications from Minoan sources that snakes were objects of veneration. The curious fact that the dragon in the *Homeric Hymn* is female can best be accounted for by the hypothesis that it is an embodiment of the goddess herself. In later accounts, as we have seen, it changes its sex to male, as no doubt a more worthy opponent for Apollo. Also it acquires the name Python, which does not appear in the *Homeric Hymn*. Another variant (first evidenced after Euripides, though it may be older in origin) represented Apollo as having to atone for the death of the serpent. His blood-guilt could only be purged by eight years' exile in Thessaly which was connected with the Delphic festival of the *Stepteria*. But this appears to be a later myth grafted on to an older ritual.[6]

The most plausible explanation, as it seems to the present writer, is that the earth-goddess was the original female deity worshipped on the site of Athena Pronaia in late Mycenaean times. Though no independent archaeological evidence exists to support it, there may have been an oracle as part of the cult. It will undoubtedly have declined, but need not have vanished completely, in the Dark Ages. Hence the arrival of Apollo as a god of divination was originally a hostile intrusion and was pictured by the worshippers of Apollo in the terms of their god's conquest of a female dragon. But later the female deities were reinstated as subordinates to Apollo. The sanctuary east of Castalia was identified with Athena Pronaia—the goddess 'in front of Apollo's temple', and beneath the terrace of Apollo's temple itself a sanctuary was assigned to Ge. There is no satisfactory archaeological evidence that this had been a place of cult in Mycenaean times. But in the classical period the legends of Apollo and his predecessors tended to be associated with it. Python was always treated as hostile, but Ge could either be regarded as the ousted occupant or else as in the Pythia's prayer in the *Eumenides* could be claimed as the first founder of a line of prophetic deities culminating in Apollo. It may have been partly with this purpose of providing the Delphic Oracle with a pedigree, that the earth-goddess, suppressed in the *Homeric Hymn*, was revived again in later legend. For in the period soon after the establishment of Apollo at Delphi when his oracle was beginning to gain recognition farther and farther beyond its immediate neighbourhood its greatest rival must have been Dodona.

The contest between the two oracles shows itself well in the development of the Argonautic legend. As we have seen, this was originally an epic of Thessaly dating back to Mycenaean times and was intimately connected with Dodona, which had supplied a branch of its oak to make the Argo speak and had sent Mopsus, one of its prophets, as a member of the crew.[7] But in the process of time, as this primitive epic travelled into southern Greece and ultimately probably to Miletus, it suffered from infiltration by Apolline influences. Mopsus was joined aboard by a second prophet, Idmon, described as a son of Apollo, and, in the literary versions of the *Argonautica* preserved for us, Jason, as it is implied, consulted the Pythia before making his expedition. Yet none of her prophecies are represented as exercising any determining influence on the course of the Argo. In fact it is evident that the connection with Delphi is superficial and probably was introduced quite late in the archaic period.

In another example taken from Greek mythology we can see both Delphi and Dodona struggling to annex to themselves a prominent character in early legend—Deucalion who, as a sort of Greek Noah, re-established the human race after a flood.[8] A fragment of Hesiod locates him in eastern Locris where in historic times traditions of him and his wife, Pyrrha, as local heroes still persisted. Delphic legend told how when this pair alone had survived the flood they came to the oracle and were told by Themis to cast the bones of their mother behind them. They solved the riddle by recognising that stones are the bones of mother earth, and the stones thus thrown turned into men and women. Thus the Delphic oracle could claim a share in restoring the human race. Also the priestly clan of the Hosioi ('The Holy Ones'), who were responsible for some of the sacred rites, traced their descent from Deucalion. But it is probable that all this was Delphic fabrication. Pindar, for instance, though he makes Deucalion's ark land on Parnassus, brings him to Locris to throw his stones and dwell there without any indication that he had consulted the Delphic oracle. In fact, in some versions Hermes conveys the instructions as the messenger of Zeus.

Dodona on its part claimed Deucalion as its own founder. After the flood he went to Epirus and consulted an oracle at the oak, and a dove sitting on the tree told him to settle on the spot. So he married Dodona, a daughter of Ocean, and with her restored the human race. These are evidently two inconsistent attempts to claim this legendary progenitor for the past history of the rival oracles.

When Dodona set its claim against Delphi it had two strong points in its favour. One was its primeval antiquity. It boasted that it was the primal oracle centre, and in so far as the question of continuity of tradition is concerned it may well have been correct. The priests of Apollo could not deny that their god had come in afterwards. Hence their only recourse was to extend Apollo's antiquity by claiming continuity with a previous oracle of the earth-goddess. It is not unlikely that she had previously given prophecies at Delphi, but if the priests were to claim her as a predecessor, they must change their attitude. They had seen Delphi's previous occupants as enemies, but now the earth-goddess and her daughter, Themis, at least, must be recognised as divine precursors of Apollo.

The other point which Dodona could urge against Delphi in its favour was that it was the oracle of Zeus himself. Apollo was at most the son of Zeus, inserted somewhat awkwardly into the Greek pantheon. On the face of it his prophecies could not be as significant as the utterances of the father of gods and men. Delphi replied with an elaborate piece of theological propaganda. While not attempting to detract from the supreme position of Zeus, it was argued that Apollo was his chosen prophet. This doctrine appears first in the *Homeric Hymn to Apollo*, but not in the sections connected with Delphi. It is in the Delian hymn where the infant god bursts from his swaddling clothes and cries:

'May the harp and the bending bow be my delight, and I shall prophesy to men the unerring will of Zeus.'[9]

In the rest of the same poem there are other references to Delos as an oracle-centre, a function which had lapsed in the classical period. But this part of the *Homeric Hymn* with its description of the Delian festival evidently dates back to an early stage of the archaic period—probably about 700 B.C.

The concept of Apollo as the prophet of Zeus may, then, have started in Delos, but it was certainly taken over and largely developed by Delphi. We find it again in the *Homeric Hymn to Hermes* which is

obviously a much later composition than the Delian hymn, and shows
evident signs of connection with the Pythian Apollo. Our limited
survivals of Greek literature do not enable us to trace it again till we
come to Pindar and the Attic dramatists. But it is a commonplace in
Aeschylus and Sophocles. For instance in the Pythia's prayer in the
Eumenides which we have already quoted as the cardinal statement of
Delphic theology, the climax of the enumeration of the prophetic
succession comes from Apollo:

'for Zeus has framed a mind inspired with mantic skill within him and has
seated him as the fourth prophet on this throne, and Loxias is the mouthpiece of his father, Zeus.'[10]

So Delphi could reply to Dodona's claims by the assertion that it
too as an oracle-centre went back to the earliest periods and that its
god stood in a special relation to Zeus. In recognising for this
purpose the divinity of the earth-goddess the Delphic priests
may also have made a further concession to their predecessors
in substituting a woman for a man as the source of prophecy. We have
already argued that the limited evidence available suggests that so
far from the Pythia being typical of archaic sanctuaries of Apollo, she
was the exception. Elsewhere the mouthpiece was normally a man.
Why, then, did Delphi show this difference? It used to be a favourite
supposition that the reason could be found in the influence of Dionysus
at Delphi.[11] There is much diffuse evidence for this Dionysiac influence
there, but it is very difficult to assess and date with any certainty. The
first author to mention Dionysus at Delphi is Aeschylus who includes
him in the Pythia's prayer in the *Eumenides*, but also pointedly treated
him as an afterthought:

'Bromios holds his place—and I do not forget him—from the time when as a
god he led the army of Bacchai and had contrived the fate of a hare for
Pentheus.'

Throughout the fifth century B.C. and thereafter references to Dionysus
at Delphi become more and more frequent. By the time of Plutarch
it was accepted that Dionysus took the place of Apollo during the
three months each winter when he was absent among the Hyperboreans.
Also, from the third century B.C. we have literary evidence for a tomb
of Dionysus within the innermost sanctuary of Apollo's temple. For
Dionysus was a god who died only to be reborn. In quite another

direction, too, the close relation of Delphi and Dionysus can be traced. As we shall see, his cult was frequently recommended in the oracular responses of the Pythia, and though some of these may be fictitious, it is likely that the Bacchic cult more than any other side of Greek religion owed its spread to Apolline influence.

In face of this array of facts it is perhaps not surprising that in the latter part of the nineteenth century scholars such as Bouché-Leclerq and Rohde attributed the whole enthusiastic element in Delphic prophecy to the influence of Dionysus. To them Apollo was typical of all that was rational, controlled and balanced in Greek thought, and Dionysus represented the emotional and unrestrained. The Pythia as an example of ecstatic prophecy did not fit with their concept of the true nature of Apollo, but could well be explained in terms of Bacchic frenzy. This also seemed to suit the circumstance that the Pythia was a woman. She could be explained as in origin a Bacchaute inspired by Dionysus, but transferred into the cult of Apollo.

On the surface this theory sounds very convincing, but examination shows that it is imaginative rather than sound in argument. For instance, though the Bacchai acquired all sorts of strange powers by the inspiration of Dionysus, our literary sources never represent them as prophesying in their frenzy. There is actually evidence for a temple of Dionysus elsewhere in Phocis with an oracle, but there the responses were given by a man, not a woman.[12] So no actual examples confirm the idea that Dionysus inspired his female devotees with prophetic powers or had any preference for a woman as his mouthpiece. In historic times the Pythia was not his medium. For in the three winter months when Apollo was absent and Dionysus remained, the oracle was closed.

The one argument which it would probably be unwise to invoke against Bouché-Leclerq and Rohde is the supposition that Dionysus like Apollo was a newcomer to Greece, and therefore could not have influenced the early practice of the Pythia. Though the evidence is not perhaps conclusive, the name of Dionysus appears to occur twice on Linear B tablets, and if this is correct, his worship, so far from being a recent importation from Asia or Thrace, may well have preceded Apollo at Delphi and elsewhere, but this fact would not prove that the Bacchic cult had any determining influence on the procedure of Apolline prophecy.

As we have already argued, the inspiration of ecstatic prophecy is a typical feature of the Apollo cult and elsewhere in primitive times was exercised through a male prophet. The choice of a woman at Delphi is the only feature that needs explanation and the hypothesis to account for it, which I prefer, is that the practice was borrowed from the previous cult of Ge and that this borrowing presumably took place at the time which we have conjectured when the earth-goddess's worship instead of being treated as hostile was accepted by the Apolline priesthood.

The earliest reference to the oracle at Delphi is presumably the passage in the *Odyssey* already discussed.[13] There Homer refers to an oracle as given by Apollo and implies, as we saw, that it contained the sort of verbal ambiguity typical later of the Pythia's utterance, but no indication otherwise is given of the method of divination employed or who was the human agent. Similarly in the *Homeric Hymn to Apollo* the god is described as 'prophesying from the laurel beneath the gorges of Parnassus'. The reference to the tree is unexplained. It may simply be topographical. It was the tree associated with Apollo, and its leaves and branches figure prominently in his worship. In historic times laurel branches were kept in the innermost sanctuary of the classical temple. So this may be a poetic way of saying 'from his shrine at Delphi'. Hiller von Gaertringen, however, preferred a much more ingenious interpretation and supposed that the laurel tree was once used as a prophetic medium at Delphi in the same way as the oak-tree at Dodona.[14] Such a theory, if it could be established, would strangely bring together the primitive practices of the two greatest oracle-centres of Greece. But there is nothing elsewhere in the cult of Apollo to confirm the hypothesis, and it is much better to suppose that the reference in the *Homeric Hymn* is vague and poetical rather than a precise description of a medium of divination. However, one does note that the writer simply mentions Apollo as prophesying, and though this would not be inconsistent with his words being uttered by the Pythia, it does not enforce that supposition. In fact, if, as we have suggested, the Pythia was borrowed from the cult of the earth-goddess, the *Homeric Hymn* with its description of the slaying of the she-dragon seems to come from an earlier stage and may be alluding to the delivering of oracles before the Pythia had been introduced into the oracular mechanism.

The earliest reference to the Pythia in literature occurs in Theognis.[15] There, addressing his boy-friend, Cyrnus, the poet describes emphatically how careful a sacred ambassador must be in reporting the message

to whom at Pytho the priestess of the god has given an oracle and signified the omen from the wealthy sanctuary.

It would be impossible to date the poem precisely, but as by its address it appears to be part of the original collection, it is probably mid sixth century in composition. The actual title 'Pythia' occurs first in Herodotus. But it is most unlikely that this lack of early evidence should be taken as pointing to a late introduction of a woman as the medium of prophecy. Our sources give no suggestion that the employment of a man in that function had ever been known at Delphi, and though this argument from silence would be rash to apply to the earliest periods it makes it most improbable that the change had taken place within the period when our traditions of the oracle are plentiful. This would seem to point to a date not later than the second half of the eighth century for the change.

What a consultation was like in such early periods it is impossible to show. Even for classical times we have no straightforward description, but have to piece together the picture from various references to details taken from authors of different dates. The practice of consulting the Delphic oracle was so completely established in classical Greece that no author thought it necessary to give a plain straightforward account of what happened. In fact, Herodotus could take for granted a knowledge of the Pythia's procedure, so that when he wanted to rebut more fantastic accounts of the operation of an oracle of Dionysus among the tribe of the Satrae in the mountainous interior of Thrace, he wrote, 'the responses are delivered by a woman as mouthpiece just as at Delphi and without anything more elaborate to it'.[16]

So at this point in our discussion it is better to postpone the question of the exact method of the oracle's operation, and simply note its general development. Greek legends particularly in their classical versions regularly introduced the Delphic oracle into the story. It could fulfil a useful function in the narrative. The hero who ultimately falls a victim to fate in spite of his efforts to avoid it could be shown as receiving an ambiguous warning from the Pythia. The hero setting out on some great adventure should go with the blessing of Apollo. The legend which ended in the establishment of some ritual practice or cult could invoke the Delphic oracle as the authority which gave the original prescript for the ceremonies. In instances such as these it is usually useless to enquire whether there was any historical foundation for this feature in the legend. Quite probably in its earliest forms the story may not have included Delphi at all. As we have seen in the myth of Deucalion, an oracle may be substituted for a message sent by Zeus through Hermes, or again the story which originally referred to an unspecified source of prophecy may later have been worked up into a specific consultation of the Pythia. None of the legends of consultations of the Delphic oracle in the prehistoric period can be safely used to reconstruct its early activities.

NOTES

1. The best summary is in P. Amandry, *La Mantique*, pp. 204 ff.
2. *Homeric Hymn to Apollo*, 388 ff. For Cretan origin of the priests: see W. G. Forrest, *Historia*, 6 (1957), p. 170; against it cf. W. Aly, *Der kretische Apollon kult* (1908) and V. von Wilamowitz-Moellendorff, *Glaube*, 2, 32
3. *Hymn*, 214 ff.
4. For a detailed discussion, see J. Fontenrose, *Python* (1959)
5. Euripides, *Iphigenia in Tauris*, 1247 ff.
6. See Parke and Wormell, *Delphic Oracle*, 1, 8
7. See Parke, *Oracles of Zeus*, 14 ff.
8. See Parke, *Oracles of Zeus*, 41 ff.
9. *Hymn*, 131 ff. and cf. 81
10. *Hymn to Hermes*, 471; Aeschylus, *Eumenides*, 19, 616 ff. and 713; Sophocles, *Oedipus Tyrannus*, 151
11. For discussions and references, see Parke and Wormell, *Delphic Oracle*, 1, 11
12. Pausanias, *10*, 23, 11
13. cf. supra p. 18
14. See Allen and Halliday's note citing Pauly-Wissowa, *4*, 25, 27 (Hiller von Gaertringen)
15. Theognis, 807
16. Hdt. *7*, 111

5

ORACLES AND COLONISATION

(I) DELPHI AND THE COLONIES

It is in the period of Greek colonisation from the last third of the eighth century that the Delphic oracle first emerges prominently in Greek history. This was particularly appropriate because of the importance and significance to the Greeks of the founding of a colony. It was not merely a great adventurous undertaking, an organised voyage of a whole flotilla over many miles of uncharted seas without a compass. Besides its secular side it was a religious innovation. The colony would need to found on its new site temples and sanctuaries of gods and heroes, and for this purpose it must carry with it the blessing of heaven. Also since Greek colonies, unlike modern colonial states, did not ordinarily have any political link with their mother city, the religious link became the more important.[1]

The colony was usually led by an individual as founder—the *oikist*—and he again could appropriately seek the approval of an oracle, not merely for the expedition and its intended site, but also for himself as its leader. For he again had a religious as well as a secular side to his position. He was the founder of cults and rituals as well as of social and political institutions, and, as the special instrument of the gods, he could look forward to a unique relation to the colony, not only at its foundation, but thereafter. On his death he could be expected to receive burial in some important place in the colony, where his grave would become the object of a heroic cult and his festival the symbol of the unity of the colony.

In view of these religious associations it is not surprising that the

foundation of many colonies was traditionally provided with a consultation of an oracle. Dodona and Ammon were said to have given
such prophetic guidance and there is some evidence that the colonies of
Miletus were sponsored by Apollo of Branchidae. But much the most
famous and frequent oracle mentioned in this connection was Delphi,
and it is probable that this general picture is correct.

If we come down to actual examples it is hard to draw the line
between original fact and later fiction. In many instances the foundation
of a colony is not only recorded as ordained by Apollo, but is tricked
out with some complicated story and completed by a response of the
Pythia in hexameter verse. Probably the actual fact of the consultation
at Delphi is not a sheer invention, though even then occasionally a
city of obscure origins may have wanted later to dignify its past
history by a suitably conventional, but picturesque beginning. More
likely the Delphic oracle had given approval, but folk tradition later
had worked it up into something more colourful than the original
facts.

Basically, the enquiry may normally have been couched in the conventional form: 'is it better and more good that the people of such and
such a city found a colony in such and such a place?' This would only
require the utterance of Apollo's assent. But our stories usually treat
the matter more picturesquely. The Pythia is made to describe the
place to be chosen and, while the description is sometimes simple and
factual, at others it is filled out with some ingenious periphrasis whose
ambiguity, like a riddle, has to be solved successfully by the enquirer.
At other times again the interest of the story tends to centre on the
oikist. A conventional motive makes him come to the oracle for quite
another purpose: particularly to enquire for a cure for some physical
disability; and this is promised to him in return for his leading the
colony as directed by Apollo.

Apart from their lively interest the value of these stories was that
they suggested that much of the initiative of the foundation lay with
the oracle. It selected the site in advance or it chose the founder, and
in each instance an inherently improbable choice proved right in the
event. But one may well question whether this was actually how the oracle
functioned, and whether, as some scholars have supposed, Delphi
became a sort of clearing-house of information on colonial development. Through previous enquiries from founders and the tales of

travellers to the shrine the priests, according to this theory, collected and organised information which then came out in the Pythia's responses.

Though we need not reduce to nothing the knowledge of the Delphic priesthood or their possible guidance to enquirers, it seems more likely that the initiative, the selection of the founder and the bulk of the information all came originally from the mother city. The sacred embassy sent to Delphi was not meant merely to acquire a bald assent from Apollo. If the response could take the form of a discursive prophecy in hexameter verse, it would no doubt be a great help to the morale of those taking part in the expedition, and before it was over and the colony safely founded, they might need all the spiritual support which they could get.

For examples of the kind of material preserved in our tradition we may take first a couple of instances of responses which at least have quite a strong possibility of being authentic. Pausanias, in connection with the legend that the river Alpheus in the Peloponnese emerged again in Sicily in the spring Arethusa, quotes the first three lines of what he describes as Apollo's prophecy when he sent Archias to found Syracuse (traditional date, 733 B.C.).[2]

'A certain Ortygia lies in the misty deep opposite Thrinacia, where the mouth of Alpheus bubbles, mingled with the springs of fair-flowing Arethusa.'

These introductory lines defined the site of Syracuse, and presumably the response went on to direct Archias, perhaps by name, to lead a colony there. The intended location was undoubtedly already known to Greek travellers, for the name, Arethusa, given to the remarkable gushing fountain of drinking-water near the seashore, had been transferred to it from a famous fountain in Euboea. So the site of the future Corinthian colony had already been prospected by Chalcidians. The notion that the spring came under the sea all the way from the river Alpheus in the Peloponnese may seem absurd to modern readers, but was not more fantastic than many similar explanations of the courses of rivers believed by the Greeks. The legend may actually have been a detail invented by the Delphians. But probably the choice of the site was already determined before the oracle was consulted and it only remained for Apollo to express his approval in appropriate hexameters.

It is interesting that in the case of Syracuse there is preserved also another foundation legend connecting it with a different Delphic response. This was evidently based on the belief that Syracuse in Sicily and Croton in south Italy were founded in the same year. The two prospective founders, Archias of Corinth and Myscellus of Achaea, consult the Pythia simultaneously.[3] The Pythia's reply was to offer them alternatives:

'You have come with a folk who are settling in a town and a country, and you would ask Phoebus to what land you are to go. But come now, point out which of the two blessings you would choose, whether to have wealth of possessions or health which gives great enjoyment.'

Faced with the decision Myscellus chose health and Archias wealth. So the god assigned Syracuse to Archias and Croton to Myscellus as the sites for their colonies, and Croton became famous for its healthy situation and the ability of its doctors: while Syracuse grew to be the wealthiest city among all the Greek colonies. Obviously this legend was invented long afterwards, when the different characteristics of the places had been developed and chronographers had worked out the synchronism.

A colony whose history illustrates well the relations of Delphi to such foundations is Cyrene. It was colonised from Thera about 630 B.C., and was originally on a small scale as an undertaking, but quite probably had the blessing of Apollo from its beginning.[4] The original response of the Pythia is not preserved, but instead in several versions a legend which turns on the motive that the founder, Battus, was selected by the oracle for the task. The Cyrenaean version told how he was feeble-voiced and stammering from birth (which the name, Battus, suggested in Greek) and went to Delphi to ask for a cure. The Pythia replied:

'Battus, you have come for a voice. But King Phoebus Apollo sends you as a founder of a colony in Libya, the nurse of flocks.'

Here we have the favourite motive of the improbable *oikist* selected by the god. The story worked out to a proper ending. When Battus reached Africa, he met a lion in the desert, and the shock caused him to utter a shout of alarm after which his speech remained clear.

Herodotus already recognised a fictitious element in the legend. As he points out Battus was the Libyan title for king and evidently was only acquired by the founder after he had reached Africa and established the colony with a monarchic constitution. As Pindar knew the founder's real name was Aristoteles, and evidently all the story of his stammer, the Pythia's response and the cure by shock treatment were all fictitious developments of the idea that Battus implied defective speech. A later version of the oracular response than that quoted by Herodotus extends the poem from two to nine lines and makes it not merely a command to colonise Libya, but a prophecy of the founding of the royal dynasty. It is evidently a piece of propaganda produced late in the sixth century when the kings of Cyrene were finding it difficult to maintain their position.

Probably there had been some original enquiry at Delphi which had authorised the foundation, but this had been overlaid by these later legendary versions. The continued connection between the colony and the oracle is well illustrated by a couple of instances, which are probably fully authentic. About 550 B.C. the Cyrenaeans decided to strengthen their numbers by inviting Greeks in general to join the colony and offered fresh allotments of land for settlers. The Pythia had evidently been asked to give Apollo's blessing to the endeavour, and two lines of her response survive which would make an excellent slogan.

'And whoever comes to lovely Libya too late for all allotment of land, I say that he will indeed regret it.'

Here we need not suppose that any original initiative came from the Delphic priests. In a later instance they may, however, have exercised some guidance. In the following reign the Cyrenaean state was in political difficulties and sent to Delphi asking how they could establish their constitution best and live well. The Pythia, as we are told, bade them bring in an arbitrator from Mantinea in Arcadia, and at the request of the Cyrenaeans the men of Mantinea selected one of their citizens named Demonax who reformed the Cyrenaean constitution on more democratic lines. Here it is likely that the choice of Mantinea as the source of a sensible arbitrator was entirely the work of the Delphic authorities.

Thus we see how Delphi both became concerned in the great expansion of Greek civilisation which was the result of the period of colonisation and also formed links with many new cities which lasted through succeeding centuries. The sequence of the enquiries recorded in our literary tradition shows a very plausible pattern of the development of the Delphic oracle's sphere of influence. In the eighth century the only colonies which are described as founded on the Pythia's instructions are situated in Sicily and south Italy and were dispatched from states in the near neighbourhood of Delphi, such as Achaea, Corinth, Sparta or at the farthest Euboea. From the beginning of the seventh century some enquirers come from the Aegean Islands—Paros, Thera and Rhodes—and they are sent not only to the West, but to North Africa and off the coast of Thrace. It is not until the latter part of the seventh century that prospective colonists came to consult the Delphic oracle from Asia Minor, and even then they seem to have been few. The gradual spread of the Pythia's influence in two centuries is quite in accordance with historic probability.

The colonisation of other regions may also have had its oracular authority elsewhere. For example, the many important colonies of Miletus in the Hellespontine region and the Black Sea coast are never associated with Delphi, except one founded by exiles. They have frequent connections with Apollo, but there is no evidence to assume that this was the Pythian god. In the temple of Branchidae in its own territory Miletus had a great Apolline oracle whose responses for these periods are almost entirely lost, but there are faint indications from later times that this was the source of the authority for the Milesian colonies.[5]

It is interesting to speculate whether there may have been a special reason in the case of one western colony why it is never described as founded in accordance with a Delphic reponse. This is Cumae, traditionally the oldest of all the Greek settlements on the Italian mainland (757 B.C.). It might be argued that its colonisation took place a little earlier than the time when the practice of consulting Delphi became established and that its Euboean and Asiatic founders might not yet have recognised the prestige of the Pythian Apollo. But there may also have been another reason, for Cumae, unlike any other Greek colony, had a prophetess of its own—the Sibyl.

(2) THE SIBYL

This brings us to one of the greatest problems in Greek divination. The Sibyl was the favourite type of prophetess in the later Greek tradition, but her earlier forms and origin are wrapped in obscurity. Her name first appears in the philosopher Heraclitus (*c.* 500 B.C.), who is quoted by Plutarch to prove the point that prophecy did not need literary grace:

'But Sibylla with frenzied mouth speaking words without smile or charm or sweet savour reaches a thousand years by her voice on account of the god.'

So to Heraclitus, as to other early writers, the Sibyl was a single prophetess of that name. Also he pictures her as inspired to ecstatic frenzy 'on account of the god', and his reference to a thousand years seems to date her long before his own day. Of Attic writers she first appears in Aristophanes in the *Peace* where he is indulging in his usual mockery of oracle mongers, and once more she is still singular. It is not till the latter half of the fourth century B.C. that Heraclides Ponticus, a pupil of the Academy, but a very imaginative writer, mentions more than one Sibyl. Also in him first they have personal names and local habitations, for he wrote of a sibyl of Erythrae in Asia Minor, called Herophile. After his time the number of these prophetesses and their identities multiplied until late writers listed as many as ten different sibyls of various places all over the known world. These are not described as contemporary with the writer nor as living in the historic period, but rather as figures of the distant past, but their work survived as it was believed, in the form of traditional prophecies, and the Sibylline oracles which are preserved in our manuscripts represent one version of this pseudonymous literature.[6]

The usual legends about the Sibyl bring her into relations with Apollo, but it is a love-hate relationship reminiscent of the story of Cassandra. As Ovid tells it, she might have had immortality at the price of yielding her virginity to the god.[7] Actually he asked her to name her wish which would be granted, and she asked to live as many years as the grains in a handful of sand. Her prayer was fulfilled, but she had failed to ask for youth. So she was fated to live for a thousand years and shrink to tiny size before her end. Ovid may appear to be a late source for the story, but it is obviously a folk tale of very primitive origin. Heraclitus' reference to a thousand years in connection with the Sibyl may derive from this legend. Also it is easy to note how it combines two motives both of which occur in the Trojan cycle, though not in Homeric contexts. One, as we have already remarked, is the motive from the legend of Cassandra of the gift obtained from Apollo as a price for virginity, which, when the bargain is unfulfilled, carries its own penalty. The other is the motive of the Tithonus legend that the gift of countless years of life is useless without the gift of youth.

These legendary connections are likely not to be accidental. The Sibyl probably had an origin in Asia Minor. Her name is usually regarded as not Hellenic.[8] Her earliest traditional locations are at Marpessus in the Troad or at Erythrae in Ionia. It is reasonable then to recognise in them some form of local prophetess, which as an institution preceded the arrival of the Greeks. At Erythrae, at least, and also, as we shall see, at Cumae in Italy, the Sibyl was associated with a cavern, and we may at once ask whether she is not yet another version of the earth-goddess's prophetess who enters a cave so as to have closer contact with the deity who inspires her. In classical times the Sibyl appears to have been thought of as deriving her inspiration from Apollo. But she is not simply the god's mouthpiece. The legends, as we have said, illustrate a love-hate relationship and in the Sibylline oracles whether from quotations or in the late collection the Sibyl speaks in her own person. When the Pythia says 'I' she means Apollo, but the Sibyl's personality was not submerged in her ecstatic utterances.

It is interesting, then, to find the Sibyl with her Asiatic origin appearing in Italy in the early Greek colony of Cumae. The most likely explanation is that when the colony was founded by the combined efforts of Chalcis, Eretria and Cyme the last of these three supplied not only the name to the colony, but also this element from the cults of Asia Minor. There appears to be no independent evidence that there had been originally a sibyl located at the Aeolian Cyme. But whether there was or whether the Aeolian colonists borrowed the idea from further afield in Asia Minor, it is highly probable that they were responsible for the establishment of the Sibyl in Italy.

There the prophetess appears in the Roman tradition in one special function as the source of the Sibylline books. These written prophecies were preserved by the Roman state as a confidential archive which could be consulted like an oracle at times of uncertainty. The legend of their origin told how the Sibyl as an aged woman came to Tarquinius Superbus and offered him nine volumes of prophecies at a high price.[9] When he refused she departed and burned three of them and later returned and offered him six for the same price. When sent away with mockery she repeated the operation returning this time with only three, and at last the king, grasping that he was rejecting a priceless opportunity, bought the remaining books for the original price. This story was evidently part of the conventional matter of the Roman annalistic tradition and may be taken as proving that the collection of poems in Greek hexameters had been acquired by the Roman state before the fall of the Monarchy. The earliest recorded instances of their consultation date under the Republic in the early fifth century as the authority for the foundation of various temples to Greek deities. The character of the divine instructions alleged to be derived from the books is generally agreed to fit plausibly with the view that they were a corpus of Greek prophecies quite probably derived from Cumae.

Neither in Asia Minor nor in Italy is there any record of the consultation of a sibyl at an oracle centre in historic times. In fact, if it were not for Vergil's superb description in *Aeneid*, Book Six, of Aeneas' visit to the Sibyl at Cumae, one would be inclined to say that sibyls were not consulted like oracles, but simply produced (or were imagined to have produced) long discursive prophecies whose application was the subject of occasional interpretation down the ages. Certainly this is the effect which they had on historical periods. But material remains of a very puzzling kind at Cumae raise the question whether there at least there had not once been an oracular establishment.

Vergil tells how the side of the rocks at Cumae was deeply cut into to form a cave from which a hundred doorways opened and carried out in confused utterance the voice of the Sibyl in prophecy. A cavern of this sort was evidently known to the poet who lived not far away in Naples, and it appears in various descriptions of geographers and travellers all writing after Vergil had popularised the identification. In the eighteenth and nineteenth centuries it was usually supposed to be the same as a large cutting in the hillside, which appears to be of Roman construction and connected with the many works in this neighbourhood of the Augustan age. But it was the achievement of Amedeo Maiuri in 1932 to find and clear out a quite different cavern, which is obviously that which Vergil had in mind. It consists of a passageway nearly 150 yards in length, some eight feet wide and sixteen feet high of a curious trapezoidal section narrowing towards the top. This vast *dromos* ends in a room, lit by a window on the right and on the left leading into an inner chamber. On either side of the doorway into this inner sanctum are rock-cut benches. Also along the passage-way, which runs parallel to the cliff, are on the right side a series of six openings at regular intervals. These with the window of the main room are evidently the 'hundred entrances' through which Vergil pictured the Sibyl's voice as issuing. Of course, in actual practice, if she is to be pictured as prophesying from the innermost chamber, it would be impossible for her voice to carry effectively through the full length of the passage to the further windows and the entrance door. But this only proves what one might already have conjectured that Vergil's vivid description is not based on any recent practice of consultation, but is largely imaginary apart from the existence of the material remains.[10]

The *Aeneid* can be taken as proving that in the last century B.C. Maiuri's cavern was open and was pointed out as the grotto of the Cumaean Sibyl. Unfortunately Maiuri's excavation failed to find any inscribed material or positive evidence for dating the construction of the cavern. He rightly called attention to the complete difference of technique and design from the Roman tunnels which are common in the neighbourhood. The walls are smooth cut in perfectly regular sections and with no use of bricks as reinforcement. All this certainly suggests, as Maiuri proposed, archaic Greek construction, though in the end, with perhaps excess of caution, he dated it to the fifth century B.C. The problem is complicated by the evident re-use of the cavern for various purposes. Maiuri himself allowed for alterations in the inner room in the fourth or more probably the third century B.C. and in later Roman times the passage was altered to adapt it for a water-cistern and in Christian times it was also used for burials. Hence it is extremely difficult to get back to its original date and function.

Our literary sources only reproduce the Vergilian tradition, except for a teasing passage in Strabo, where he quotes Ephorus, the fourth-century historian, on the location of Homer's Cimmerians at the lake Avernus.[11] He described them as

dwelling in subterranean houses which are called 'Argillae' and going to and fro to each other by certain excavations and receiving foreigners into the oracle-centre which is situated far underground. They live from mining and from those consulting the oracle and the king had assigned to them some contributions. It was an ancestral custom to those connected with the prophetic shrine that none of them should see the sun, but go out of the caverns by night.

This, as Ephorus explains, was why Homer in the *Odyssey* could describe the Cimmerians as never looked on by the sun. He adds that

later they were blotted out by a certain king because an oracle response had not been fulfilled for him, but the oracle-centre still persists after it had transferred to another place.

The Cimmerians like gnomes living in subterranean mines are very improbable creatures whom we do not hear of from other authors. The most suspicious circumstance is that after having described their underground life Ephorus explains that they are not existent any longer. This makes it likely that they were a purely fictitious people. The one element of his account which Ephorus states is still surviving is the oracle-centre, which while removed to another place, is presumably still to be pictured as underground. If so, one may wonder whether this is to be taken as a reference from the fourth century B.C. to the oracular grotto of the Sibyl.

When faced with a peculiar work of human effort, such as this vast subterranean tunnel with its chambers, the archaeologist is likely to conjecture a religious function, and here this conjecture is no doubt correct. One must assume, as already suggested, that the Greek settlers brought with them from Asia Minor a practice still existent there in the mid-eighth century B.C. but fated to die long before classical times. For the purpose of prophecy a woman should enter a cave. But presumably at Cumae no suitable natural formation was available. So at some time in the archaic period the present grotto was elaborately constructed. It would appear as though the Sibyl, if we may so call her, traversed the full length of the corridor to reach the holy of holies. On the way she passed a recess on the left which may have been contrived from earliest times to provide a bath for purificatory ablutions. The benches outside the door of the innermost sanctum suggest that she was accompanied by priestly assistants or enquirers or both, who remained seated without while she completed the prophetic ritual within. So much may be conjectured, but we have no literary tradition to guide us. Evidently the use of the cavern as an oracle-centre must have ceased at quite an early date. The flourishing period of Cumae was under its tyrant Aristodemus, in the latter part of the sixth and the early part of the fifth century B.C. In 438 or 421 B.C. it fell to the Samnites and one might wonder whether the Sibyl ceased to function as an oracle-centre then. Ephorus in the mid-fourth century seems to write as if something still persisted, if he is alluding to Cumae. But certainly by the time that the Romans occupied Campania (334 B.C.) there is no indication that they found a prophetess in action. If the oracle-centre was already defunct, this would explain why Vergil three centuries later is evidently drawing on folklore and poetic imagination in reconstructing the scene.

Alternatively he suggested elsewhere in the *Aeneid* another form of consultation—by means of writing.[12] The Sibyl wrote her prophecy on the leaves of trees and arranged them in the cavern (presumably on the floor) in the proper order to make sense and left them. But when the enquirers entered the draught from the door blew the leaves about the cave so that it was impossible to recover the correct arrangement and the sense of the oracle. It is not known whether Vergil in this vivid narrative is describing any actual form of consultation. Nothing exactly similar is known elsewhere. It may simply be another piece of folklore, particularly as it ends with the scene of the enquirers departing disappointed. For popular imagination liked to visualise the Sibyl frustrating those who consulted her. The Sibyl of Cumae must remain for the modern enquirer an equally mysterious being in herself.

NOTES

1. For the latest discussions of Delphi and colonisation: see Parke and Wormell, *Delphic Oracle*, *1*, 49 ff. and W. G. Forrest, *Historia*, 6 (1957), 160 ff. For the relations of mother-city and colony: see A. J. Graham, *Colony and Mother City* (1964)

2. Pausanias, *5*, 7, 3 (Parke and Wormell, *2*, no. 2)

3. Strabo, *6*, 2, 4 (Parke and Wormell, *2*, no. 229)

4. Parke and Wormell, *1*, 73 ff., and *2*, no. 38–42, 69 and 71

5. Cf. e.g. Rehm, *Das Delphinion in Milet*, no. 155

6. Heraclitus, *fr.* 92 (Diels) — Plutarch, *Moralia* 397A, Aristophanes, *Peace*, 1047 ff.; Heraclides Ponticus, Mueller, *Fragmenta Historicorum Graecorum*, vol. II, 197

7. Ovid, *Metamorphoses*, *14*, 132

8. But H. T. Wade-Gery has called my attention to such terminations as Arist*yllos* and Is*yllos* and to such a root as *Siby*rtios

9. Dionysius of Halicarnassus, *Antiquities*, *4*, 62 and various later references

10. Vergil, *Aeneid*, *6*, 42 ff. and A. Maiuri, *The Phlegraean Fields*, 123 ff.

11. Strabo, *5*, 4, 5; Jacoby, *Fragmente der Griechischen Historiker*, 70 ff., 134

12. Vergil, *Aeneid*, *3*, 444

6

DELPHI IN THE EARLY ARCHAIC PERIOD

(1) KINGS, TYRANTS AND POETS

If we go back to Delphi, we noted last that while her early enquirers came from the Peloponnese or at farthest Euboea it was not till well into the seventh century that the states of Asia Minor consulted the Pythia. This was true, as far as is known, with regard to colonies. But in other connections Delphi's fame may have early reached Asia. For by the beginning of the seventh century B.C. the practice had begun of an oriental monarch making a dedication at Delphi, presumably to win the favour of Apollo in his dealings with the Greeks. Herodotus mentions that

Midas, son of Gordius, king of Phrygia had dedicated the royal throne on which he used to sit in judgment, an object worth notice.

No legend of an enquiry by Midas survives, and some modern scholars have been sceptical about the genuineness of the object. But recent American excavations in the Phrygian capital—Gordium—have shown what a magnificent culture existed there, evidently with considerable contacts with the Greeks, and it is most likely that Midas had trading and diplomatic dealings with Hellas itself.[1]

The relations of Lydia with Delphi are not open to the same degree of doubt. Gyges, the first king of the new dynasty of Mermnades, who came to the throne in Sardis about 675 B.C., sent considerable offerings of gold to Delphi. The popular story there later was the oracle had been called in to arbitrate between him and his political opponents, and had decided in favour of Gyges, who had shown an appropriate gratitude. It is somewhat too improbable that the Lydians themselves at such a date could have referred their sovereignty to the decision of the Pythian Apollo. At most he may have been induced to deliver an approving oracle which strengthened the new claimant to the Lydian throne in Greek eyes. The Delphians went further and claimed that the Pythia also had prophesied that the dynasty would last for five generations and that this forecast was not regarded till it was fulfilled by the fall of Croesus. Here we have what is obviously a *post eventum* prophecy linked conveniently to the establishment of Gyges in power.[2]

Delphi also became associated with the early Greek tyrants. Like oriental kings they were in a position to be generous in their offerings to Apollo and also might be glad to win favourable responses from the oracle, which were likely to help to justify the rather unconstitutional powers of the autocrat. It need not be supposed that the first tyrants were generally regarded with bitter hatred outside the ranks of the oligarchs whom they displaced. So in their own day the oracle may have seen no grave objection to recognising them. In later times, as the idea of tyranny became more and more objectionable in itself, the part played by the Pythia was pictured in accordance with this view. So one favourite type of legend represented the oracle as foretelling the emergence of the tyrant or greeting him before he had shown himself. Also the prophecy might be worded so as to convey, as in the response about Gyges, an indication how long the dynasty would last. None of these responses are likely to be completely authentic both in contents and in context. For instance the alleged prophecies of Cypselus' birth may well have been invented in his honour and to the greater glory of Apollo after he had made himself tyrant of Corinth, but still in his lifetime. The lines in which the Pythia appears to address him spontaneously, calling him 'blessed' and describing him as a king, may actually have been delivered to him in person after he had achieved power. For Cypselus showed his devotion to Apollo by constructing at Delphi the first treasury dedicated to the god. These buildings took the form of miniature temples and besides honouring the deity with a consecrated building provided a convenient place in which to concentrate the valuable dedications of one community. Cypselus originally put his own name on the treasury as dedicator. So he regarded it as a personal offering. It was only after the fall of his dynasty that the

Delphians allowed the Corinthians to substitute the city's name in place of the tyrant's. Perhaps it was when Cypselus visited Delphi to dedicate his treasury that the Pythia addressed him in honorific terms. If so, the response was later altered by the addition of a third line which foretold power for him and his son but not for the next generation.[3]

Delphi in her relations with the tyrants need not be regarded as originally intending to support one kind of political ideology against another, but it is quite possible that already before the end of the seventh century the oracle had been asked to support the reformation of a constitution. In the poems of Tyrtaeus occurred a description how some Spartans, unspecified in our present text,

heard from Phoebus and brought from Pytho homeward the oracles of god and the words which reach fulfilment.[4]

He follows with instructions for operating a constitution consisting of kings, elders and commons, which evidently corresponds with the prose document quoted by Plutarch as the chief *Rhetra* of Lycurgus. In later Greek times from early in the fourth century B.C. it was usual enough to suppose that Lycurgus was a historic person who had gone to Delphi and received from the Pythia the form of the Spartan constitution. It would appear that Tyrtaeus did not tell the story in this personal form. In fact he may even have left it vaguely unstated whether the enquiry at Delphi was made by contemporary Spartans or by their distant ancestors. The whole question of the constitutional change in Sparta and its date is still the subject of lively controversy, but whether or not the *Rhetra* was actually authorised by the Pythia evidently as early as the time of Tyrtaeus it was believed that this was so, and Delphi came to occupy a very special position in relation to the Spartan state. For instance the Spartans in Herodotus' day told a legend to explain the dual kingship as established by the Delphic oracle after twin sons had been born posthumously to King Aristodemus. Also the kings in historic times had associated with each of them two Spartans known as Pythii. They were sacred ambassadors who were nominated to go to Delphi wherever an enquiry had to be made, and when in Sparta their function was to preserve the oracles which had already been delivered. Sparta was the only state which is known to have maintained a standing commission of this sort.

So far the only oracular enquiries which we have discussed came from states or kings and tyrants speaking in the name of their states. It is typical of our literary sources on which we depend for the bulk of our evidence that these are the kind of subjects which they mention. But actually it is unlikely that even the major oracle-centres at the height of their fame confined themselves to this kind of official business. Though public enquiries must have been the most important and will have taken precedence over the rest, the ordinary private enquirer must have made up numerically the largest part of the oracle's business. Such enquiries are implied in the legendary stories of the period. Eetion receives the prophecy that his son will be tyrant of Corinth when he is asking about offspring. Battus of Thera is requesting a cure for his stammer when he is sent to found Cyrene. No doubt it was true enough, as these sources implied, that private individuals consulted the Pythia on such questions as their failure to have a family or the possible cure for a physical defect. Our ancient authors would have no occasion to mention particular instances of this sort if they did not concern important historical characters.

One private enquiry from the seventh century B.C. which has come through to us concerned indirectly the poet, Archilochus, and it is his fame that has immortalised the story. His family had some connection with Delphi, because his father, Telesicles, had been nominated by the Pythia as *oikist* for the colony at Thasos, sent out from the island of Paros (early seventh century B.C.). The two lines of verse which are extant may well be authentic:

Announce to the Parians, Telesicles, that I bid found a conspicuous city on the island of Eëria.[5]

As in other instances we need not suppose that this was a spontaneous utterance, but simply that the oracle had been asked for Apollo's approval for the founder and the site. The Delphic priest chose to refer to the island of Thasos under a picturesque legendary name. There is also extant a single line enjoining Archilochus himself to settle in Thasos, but its claim to authenticity may be much more dubious.

The poet, who has sometimes been described as the first Greek whom we can recognise as an individual with a personal character, was born the child of a slave-woman, and lived a violent and restless life. At one time he settled in Thasos and fought (or ran away from) the Thracians on the mainland. At another time he was a mercenary soldier. But he seems to have returned in the end to his native Paros. Even so he died fighting, killed in battle by Callondes, a native of the neighbouring, rival island of Naxos. Through all this chequered career he had produced highly original and colourful poetry in new lyric metres. So it is not surprising that his fame had evidently reached Delphi. In later times the oracle was supposed to have prophesied his birth and have been connected with other points in his career. These are likely to be legendary tales, but one episode may be completely genuine.[6]

Some time after he had killed Archilochus, Callondes (who was himself probably a picturesque character, for he had the nickname 'The Crow') came to Delphi to consult the oracle and instead of receiving a response was expelled from the sanctuary by the Pythia who addressed him with the verse:

'You have slain the Muses' servant. Leave the temple.'

Callondes was not unnaturally taken aback at this treatment. By a procedure which has a later parallel he returned later in the day as a suppliant and appealed for Apollo's pardon, while arguing (not unjustly) that he had killed Archilochus in fair fight. The god refused to accept this as a complete justification, but instructed Callondes to go and appease the spirit of Archilochus at Taenarum, where there was an ancient sanctuary for communication with the dead.

It is a strange story and in later times classical scholars were puzzled why Apollo should show such consideration for a man of the highly dubious moral character of Archilochus. But it is to some extent the very improbability of the tale that makes it unlikely that it was simply invented, and one feature fits most appropriately with the third quarter of the seventh century B.C. This is the concern over blood-guilt and purification.

(2) BLOOD-GUILT

Between the Homeric and the archaic age took place a transition in Greek thought and religious practice, which Professor Dodds has described in terms of a change from a shame-culture to a guilt-culture.[7] In Homer the slaying of a man, provided he was not a near kinsman, was not thought of so much in terms of impurity incurred as of the blood-price to be paid or, if there was not this material compensation, the physical vengeance of the dead man's kin. By the archaic period this treatment of manslaughter as a matter to be settled between families was replaced by a general recognition by communities that the shedding of blood was in itself polluting and that the slayer not only on his own account, but also for the sake of those with whom he came in contact, must be treated as under a curse from the gods. Apollo, who was greatly regarded as the god of purity, may have been partly responsible for this change of attitude. But it is even more likely that the Delphic oracle was instrumental in spreading the remedy for blood-guilt—ritual purification.

In the mythology of ritual Delphi is particularly associated with two motives. One is human sacrifice which appears in the legends in two opposite forms. Sometimes the story tells of the sacrifice or intended sacrifice of the king's son or daughter. The occasion is treated as isolated and extraordinary and is not made the foundation for a succession of regular offerings of this kind of victim. The Delphic oracle in such legends is made the appropriate authority for this peculiar deed, and one may suppose that it has no historic foundation and even that the oracle was simply introduced as a convenient piece of the machinery of telling the story convincingly.[8] For a king's son or daughter to be sacrificed it was not sufficient to say that it was the will of the gods, it had to be shown why this should be believed.

The oracle's other function in the myths of human sacrifice is in connection with the replacement of this grisly ritual by some milder offering in substitution. Here it is possible that there is an actual historical foundation to the story. In some instances it is quite probable that there had been a primitive ritual of human sacrifice and that it had later been replaced by something less savage. Also it would at least be likely that authority for the change might have been sought at an oracle. The examples preserved in mythology are too uncertain historically for one to have any confidence that any particular instance is founded on a genuine response of the Pythia, but at least it is not impossible, nor in any way inconsistent with the attitude which seems to have been typical of the Delphic authorities in the archaic period.[9]

This point is further emphasised by the part which the oracle plays in Greek myths dealing with blood-guilt and purification. In the form in which the Pythia is concerned in them they are post-Homeric and belong to the later era of the guilt-culture. For example, Orestes appears in the *Odyssey*, where he is mentioned several times, as a son who is bound in duty to demand blood for blood from his mother's lover and his father's murderer, Aegisthus, and no oracle is given to encourage him. This was doubtless the primitive version dating from the time when a blood-feud was recognised as an institution. By the time of the Attic tragedians this attitude had completely changed, and the Delphic oracle is introduced into the legend as the source of a response which either approves Orestes' intention or even threatens him if he fails to avenge his father. With this change comes an added stress on the slaying of Clytemnestra, Orestes' own mother, a deed which, though implied in Homer, was there left without emphasis. Also Apollo does not merely approve the vengeful plans of Orestes in advance, he also purifies the matricide after the deed. Delphi was only one of various places in Greece which possessed rituals of purification and claimed Orestes as a distinguished client. In fact so far as Delphi was concerned the two ideas may have gone together. For Apollo could most reasonably be expected to purify Orestes if he had first encouraged him to shed blood. With this link with the oracle went also a localisation of the legend in Phocis, as the scene of his refuge abroad when a child. Homer gave no place-names, except for describing him once as coming 'from Athens' to the murder. Later legends described how he was brought up at the court of King Strophius and there met the king's son, Pylades, who was to be his faithful companion thereafter.[10]

Parallel to the legend of Orestes is that of Alcmaeon. He, too, slew his mother because of her guilty responsibility for his father's death. Legend made him consult Delphi and receive Apollo's approval in advance, and also after his blood-guilt the oracle advised him not to return to his native land, but to settle on a place which had not been seen by the sun at the time of the murder, as all the rest of the world was polluted. The solution of this puzzling command was found by his occupying some of the freshly deposited alluvial soil at the mouth of the river Achelous. This oracle was similar to Orestes' wanderings after his murder, and was a favourite Delphic motive as is shown by the fact that it was even applied to Apollo himself. The myth was told that Apollo had had to suffer nine years' exile in atonement for slaying Python. Again it occurred as a motive in connection with the *oikists* of colonists. The Pythia designates an enquirer such as Leucippus who has come to seek atonement for murdering his father. The settlement overseas would on this theory produce purification.[11]

These examples from mythology show how in such a period as the seventh century B.C. Delphi was deeply concerned in the question of blood-guilt. In contrast to the early age it recognised and was fully conscious of the existence of this pollution, but also it was prepared to offer purifications and atonements. These are the exact circumstances in which the strange episode of the Slayer of Archilochus took place.

(3) THE FIRST SACRED WAR

By the end of the seventh century Delphi was no doubt a place of considerable importance and much accumulated wealth, as it was reckoned in those archaic times. Presumably already, perhaps quite long before, there had been composed those strangely allusive lines in which Achilles is made to refer in the *Iliad* to

'all that the stone threshold of the archer keeps within, the threshold of Phoebus Apollo at rocky Pytho.'[12]

It was somewhat strange that this important sanctuary with its growing accumulation of offerings was attached to a small village perched high on a mountain slope. Even as late as the early fourth century B.C. it is clear that Delphi did not contain a thousand male citizens of full age and in the seventh century the number was probably far less. At that period the prominent place in the neighbourhood was Crisa, a town situated between Delphi and the sea. The precise site of the archaic town has not been found. But it evidently was so placed as to take advantage of two great sources of wealth. The valley of the Pleistos and of the Hylaithos converged to form a fruitful plain which was at the end of an inlet giving convenient access to the Corinthian gulf. It is significant that this waterway itself had at one time borne the name 'Crisaean Gulf'.[13] Evidently in early times Crisa had rivalled Corinth as a place of importance on its coasts. Also it had been concerned in one at least of the settlements in south Italy. By its situation at the head of the Gulf of Itea, Crisa commanded the approach to Delphi from the sea and it may also have controlled the routes down the valley from Amphissa, leaving only the high pass from Lebadeia, the Cloven

Way used by Laius, outside its hold. So though it is likely that Delphi was always a separate political unit, a small village like many others in Phocis, Crisa by its size and wealth and by its strategic position must have tended to threaten the independence of its small neighbour.

At a date traditionally assigned to 591 B.C. Crisa was taken as a result of the First Sacred War, and was razed to the ground. The circumstances that led to this dramatic conclusion are highly obscure. The war resulted in the situation that the Delphians were made a politically independent community, but the sanctuary and its chief festival were controlled by a religious league—the Amphictyony. It was this body which had waged war against Crisa in the name of Delphi. Such religious leagues were a feature of early Greece, and it is evident that the Amphictyony had a history reaching back far into the past before it came to Delphi. One obvious sign of its antiquity is the fact that its members were officially grouped not as city-states, but as tribes, and its origin evidently dated from the time before the city-state as a political unit had been evolved. Its original centre had not been at Delphi, but at the temple of Demeter at Anthela near Thermopylae, and the terminology of some of its official titles dated from that stage.[14] Evidently by the end of the seventh century Thessaly was dominant in the league, as a majority of the tribes were part of that state or its periphery.

Our sources represent the Thessalians as leading the attack on Crisa, but other powers such as Athens and the tyrant Cleisthenes of Sicyon succeeded in taking a hand in the struggle. The Athenian claim to membership of the Amphictyony was based on the fact that one of the tribes included was the Ionians—evidently originally the Euboeans facing Anthela across the strait. But in historic times Athens occupied one of their two seats. Similarly Cleisthenes could claim to be Dorian and the central Greek state of Doris had two places originally. It seems preferable to the present writer to suppose that the Amphictyony had already managed to acquire a position at Delphi in the seventh century and this view fits with some indications from Greek mythology.

The problem about the First Sacred War is whether to accept the implication of our ancient authorities that already before the war the Amphictyony had been concerned with Delphi or to follow some modern scholars who reconstruct the history on the theory that the war itself was the first occasion for Thessaly to thrust its influence so far south.[15] The Delphians may have been glad enough to invite the Anthela Amphictyony to meet at Apollo's sanctuary and use their prestige as a counterpoise to Crisa's dominance. In any case by the beginning of the sixth century the two rivals with an interest in the sanctuary—the religious league and the nearest city-state—clashed in war. The Amphictyony declared a crusade against Crisa for offences against Apollo's pilgrims or his property. (Our later sources give vague trumped-up charges.) Crisa was destroyed, and Delphi came under the protection of the religious league. Its delegates came twice yearly to Delphi and exercised control over the sanctuary and its buildings. They instituted a great four-yearly festival, the Pythian games, and declared the fertile lands of Crisa accursed so that they could never be cultivated.

Thus the Delphians came to occupy a position unique in Greece. They ceased to be reckoned as members of their old tribal unit, the Phocians, and stood apart from any local association. They owned no extensive lands, but lived off the profits of the temple and its visitors. They acquired a kind of Panhellenic status through the inter-tribal structure of the Amphictyony. At the same time they retained complete control of the oracle itself. The priestly officials continued to be drawn exclusively from the Delphians. It is not surprising, then, that the Pythian oracle became even more widely recognised as the chief centre of its kind in the Greek world. Already it was probably the most famous, but hereafter its rivals were all of only local association, while Delphi could stand as the god's mouthpiece in addressing all the Greeks.

The oracle's importance is shown by its significant relations with the chief events of Greek history which followed. The era of colonisation was almost over but other developments called for oracular sanctions. For instance in Athens Solon had Apollo's support in his legislation. This may have been linked with Athens' part in the Sacred War. Sparta, which had had no part in the war, sought the god's approval for a policy of territorial expansion. The occasion was a war with Sparta's northern neighbour Tegea, which she hoped to develop into a conquest of all Arcadia. Delphi when consulted demurred from the larger programme, but in favourable but poetically obscure terms agreed to the seizure of Tegea. However the campaign ended in defeat. The Spartans were worsted, and those of them who were made

C

prisoners were compelled to work the fields of Tegea wearing the chains which they had brought to enslave the Tegeans themselves. The Delphians managed by an ingenious reinterpretation to justify the Pythia's answer as prophesying, not victory for Sparta, but this form of disaster.[16]

So Sparta, appropriately and perhaps with Delphi's advice, changed her policy completely. Instead of trying to conquer Tegea and annex its territory she set out to win it over by diplomacy. Here we encounter the first instance of a political use of ritual which became typical of Spartan propaganda. They claimed that they had secretly discovered in Tegean territory the bones of the hero, Orestes, and had removed these with Apollo's blessing to Sparta. By so doing they had, as it were, transferred the spiritual luck and leadership of the country to their own control. This curious view of the mystic power latent in the bodies of deceased heroes was widely and intensely accepted in Greek belief, and Delphi frequently made use of the idea. The Spartans themselves having acquired dominance in Tegea proceeded soon after to use the same kind of method in an attempt to spread their influence northward in Achaea.

(4) CROESUS

It was only to be expected that the rise of Delphi would attract attention even from outside the Greek world. We have already noticed how Phrygian and Lydian kings had honoured the Pythian Apollo in the past. But all their offerings were quite eclipsed by the unparalleled series of dedications sent by King Croesus of Lydia. A century after they had reached Delphi they were seen and described in detail by Herodotus, who also reproduced at length the stories which the local guides told in explanation of them.[17] They had something to explain because while the gifts which Croesus had sent to Apollo surpassed any other dedication, it was well known that his reign had ended in disaster when his kingdom was conquered by the Persians. The magnificence of the offerings and the downfall of the donor were both explained and justified by an elaborate series of oracular responses worked up into a pious legend.

It was told that Croesus conceived the plan of conquering Persia before it became any stronger, and decided first to test the oracles of the Greeks and one in north Africa to find which he could trust to advise him on this decision.[18] The method which he used was to send out at the same time ambassadors to all the sanctuaries with instructions to enquire on the hundredth day from their departure what Croesus was doing at that moment. Then they were to write down the answers and bring them back for comparison. Evidently the principle of the test was that one hundred days represented the maximum time which any of the ambassadors would take in reaching their destination, so that the same test of clairvoyance could apply to all simultaneously. The list of oracle-centres as recorded by Herodotus included, besides Delphi, Abae in Phocis, Dodona, the sanctuaries of the heroes Amphiaraus and Trophonius, and the temple of Apollo at Branchidae near Miletus, as well as the one non-Greek shrine of Ammon in Libya.

The result of the test was a complete victory for the Pythian Apollo who in the usual faintly allusive hexameters referred to the fact that Croesus had been engaged in cooking a tortoise with lamb in a bronze cauldron with a bronze lid. Also the Pythia's words included what was always quoted later as the manifesto of the god's omniscience:

'But I know the number of grains of sand and the measures of the sea, and the dumb I understand and the speechless I hear.'

After the success of the test Croesus sent his magnificent offerings to Delphi. The most notable was a lion of pure gold standing on a pyramid of one hundred and seventeen bricks of 'white gold' (an alloy of gold and silver). The weight of the lion was about a quarter of a ton. Also there were two colossal vessels, one of gold, one of silver, which stood on either side of the entrance to the temple, and in addition Herodotus lists numbers of other smaller dedications of gold and silver. There can be no doubt that Croesus was extraordinarily generous to Delphi, but this fact does not prove that he really had satisfied himself by experiment that it was the only truthful oracle. Herodotus himself was aware that Croesus had in fact given generously to other oracles in a way which was hard to reconcile with the Delphic story. For instance he knew that the sanctuary of the hero Amphiaraus had been given a shield and spear of solid gold, and still more remarkably records that he had heard that the temple of Branchidae had received dedications equal in weight and style to those at Delphi. These treasures would, of course, have been removed at the time of the Persian sack of

Miletus after the Ionian revolt, and it is possible therefore that their scale may have been exaggerated by later tradition. Still it is not likely that there had not been some considerable offerings by Croesus there too, to provide the basis of the tradition. The true position, therefore, was that, though he had been more generous to Delphi than to any other oracle, he had not treated it as unique. The story of the test with its magnificent climax in the great statement of the Pythian Apollo's powers was an invention of the Delphic priesthood built on the superb grandeur of Croesus' dedications. We may note that Herodotus had been unable to obtain a traditional version of the response of Amphiaraus in the test, though it had apparently merited a quite considerable consolation prize! Also the list of oracles consulted, if considered critically, is not an entirely probable selection. For instance, Dodona is included though there is nothing to suggest in tradition or in the material remains from the site that it was normally consulted by Ionians in the early part of the sixth century. Similarly the appearance of Ammon in the list is remarkable. Scholars who take the story at its face value regularly quote Herodotus as evidence for the earliest connection between the oracle at Siwa and the Greek world. But it would be wiser to reverse the argument and recognise that the list in its form as preserved in Herodotus probably did not date earlier than the beginning of the fifth century. This would suit with the circumstance that the first literary echo of the Pythian Apollo's manifesto occurs in Pindar's ninth Pythian ode (474 B.C.).[19] It is probable that the legend took shape not long before that date. The oracle-centres mentioned and omitted suit well with a Delphic source about that date. Dodona, as a long-standing rival in west Greece, could not be left out and by that date its consultation from Lydia would not be too unlikely. Also, Ammon through the influence of Cyrene was becoming known for the first time. Local rivals, such as Abae, Amphiaraus and Trophonius were included. But in Asia Minor the sanctuaries of Apollo at Gryneum and Claros were passed over, though it is impossible to suppose that an Asian monarch would have left them out. By the fifth century they had ceased to be of significance to the priests of Delphi. But Branchidae was too important to be omitted, and if the story was invented after its sack there would be no difficulty in having to account for generous offerings there.

If we agree that the dedications of Croesus were not sent because he had proved by experiment that the Pythian Apollo was uniquely truthful, we must explain them instead as the biggest move in a general effort on his part to win the favour of the Greeks by magnificent offerings in their sanctuaries. If so, it is likely that Herodotus was right in supposing a connection with Croesus' war against Persia. As he records the story Croesus asked if he should lead an army against the Persians and if he should associate any other army as an ally. The Pythia's reply contained the famous ambiguity that if he led the expedition he would destroy a mighty empire. It may be significant that Herodotus does not record this reply in hexameter verse, but only in prose. A century later Aristotle knew a single line of poetry which conveyed the meaning, and it may have been known also to Herodotus, but, if so, he paraphrased it in prose, perhaps feeling that the naively simple ambiguity was made less obvious in that form.[20] He also added that the Pythia advised him to find out the most powerful of the Greeks and make them his friends, thus answering his enquiry about allies. Herodotus also tells an additional story about an enquiry from Croesus about the length of his reign with an hexameter response containing a suitably metaphorical allusion to Cyrus.

Obviously these stories in the form given by Herodotus are retold after the event, but it is possible to reconstruct, conjecturing the shape of the original responses. Probably Croesus in cultivating the Pythian Apollo with great offerings and enquiring about his expedition against Persia had two interrelated objects in view. A favourable response from the oracle would be good for morale in general, and as he intended to seek the help of the Spartans to support his campaign, a direction to obtain powerful allies from the Greeks would be a great reinforcement to his diplomacy. Also we have no reason to doubt that the Delphic authorities supplied the oracular responses that were needed. Herodotus records the reference to obtaining powerful allies, and this can be accepted as authentic. As to the ambiguity about destroying a great empire, it is most unlikely that this was uttered by the Pythia in this form. Probably her reply was much less equivocal and offered Croesus the victory which he desired with no great hesitation. The favourable oracle will have been suppressed after the event and the present rather lame equivocation substituted.

It would not be surprising that the Delphic authorities encouraged Croesus in his imperialistic venture. One need not picture the priests as bribed by his offerings. The vast magnitude of the oriental monarch's wealth must have conveyed to the inhabitants of a little Greek town the feeling of boundless resources whose victory could not be questioned. It was only reasonable that the authorities of Delphi showed their gratitude and admiration by supporting their benefactor. But it must have come as a rude surprise when Croesus' campaign ended in complete disaster, and not only did his kingdom fall before Cyrus, but the victorious Persian armies swept through the Greek cities of Asia Minor. Up to this point, so far as we can tell, the Delphic oracle had never made a catastrophic blunder. The authorisation of Greek colonies was a service which did not test the prescience of the oracle severely. In the minor wars of Greek states occasionally the Pythia might seem to have promised victory to Sparta when Tegea was successful. But such errors could be explained away by reinterpreting the figurative language of a prophecy. The fall of Croesus was much worse. The pages of the wonderful *apologia* reproduced by Herodotus are an indication of the trouble which it caused the Delphic priesthood to explain away their mistake by re-telling the story. Also we may well suppose that their nerve was shaken at the disaster, and a policy of playing for safety was adopted henceforth.

The mistake in foreign policy may soon have been followed by a disaster at Delphi itself. Certainly some time after Croesus' gifts had been installed, but before the last quarter of the sixth century the temple of Apollo accidentally caught fire and was burnt to the ground. The great vessels of gold and silver standing in front of the temple were moved to a place of safety in time, but the gold lion fell from his pyramid of brick and was partially melted before the fire was stopped.[21]

The Amphictyons voted to build a new temple and probably each member state, as again in the fourth century B.C., was assessed to pay a contribution. The Delphians undertook the responsibility of raising a quarter of the amount and sent collectors round the Greek world to solicit subscriptions. Ultimately the building was completed by the Alcmaeonids in the last years of the sixth century, but a great deal was to happen before then.

NOTES

1. Herodotus, *1*, 14. cf. A. R. Burn, *The Lyric Age of Greece*, 57
2. Hdt. *1*, 13, 1 (Parke and Wormell, *Delphic Oracle 2*, no. 51)

3. Hdt. 5, 92 (Parke and Wormell, 2, no. 6, 7 and 8). The treasury, Plutarch, 3, 400E

4. Plutarch, *Lycurgus*, 6 (Parke and Wormell, 2, no. 21 with the alternative version from Diodorus). See Parke and Wormell, 1, 89 ff. and for a more recent discussion, see von Blumenthal in Pauly-Wissowa s.n. Tyrtaios

5. Oenomaus in Eusebius, *Praeparatio Evangelica*, 6, 7

6. Parke and Wormell, 1, 396 ff.

7. E. R. Dodds, *The Greeks and the Irrational*, 17 ff.

8. e.g. the legend of Phrixus and Helle: Apollodorus, 1, 9, 1 etc.

9. e.g. the cult of Dionysus Aigobolus at Thebes: Pausanias, 9, 8, 2

10. Homer, *Od.* 1, 30 ff., 298; 3, 306 ff. ('from Athens'); 4, 546; 11, 461. For the Delphic response, cf. Parke and Wormell, 2, no. 139

11. Alcmaeon: Parke and Wormell, 2, no. 202 and 204. Apollo: id, 1, 7. Leucippus: id, 1, 53

12. Homer, *Il*, 9, 404. For the population of Delphi in the early 4th century: cf. the law of Cadys, *Delph.* 1, 294–5

13. e.g. Thucydides, 1, 107, 3. For south Italy, see the reference to Metapontum, Strabo. 6, 1, 15, though Dunbabin, *Western Greeks*, 32, regarded it as unhistoric

14. Official meetings are called Pylaia and the ordinary delegates Pylagorai

15. For the Sacred War: cf. Parke and Wormell, 1, 100 ff. and (with a different interpretation) W. G. Forrest, *Bulletin de Correspondance Hellénique*, 80 (1956), 33 ff.

16. Solon: Parke and Wormell, 1, 110 ff. Sparta: id. 1, 94 ff.

17. Herodotus, 1, 50 ff.

18. Herodotus, 1, 47 ff.

19. Pindar, *Pythian Odes 9*, 44 ff.

20. Parke and Wormell, 2, no. 53 and 54

21. For the fire: Hdt. 1, 48 and Pausanias, 10, 5, 3, dating it by Attic archon-year and Olympiad to 548–7 B.C., but this is awkwardly early. For the raising of contributions: Hdt. 2, 180

7

DELPHIC PROCEDURE

(I) THE PYTHIA

Meantime it may be best to pause in our historical narrative and discuss the methods of divination used at Delphi. It seemed inappropriate to go into this question at the beginning of the account of the oracle's activity, because we have no contemporary evidence bearing directly on the subject. As we saw, the one ambiguous phrase in the *Homeric Hymn* describing the Pythian Apollo as prophesying from the laurel could be variously interpreted. Our accounts of the oracle's working, vague as they are, practically date from the fifth century. To authors writing then it was an accepted belief that the method of divination had been the same in the far past as in their own day. Whether they were correct in this we cannot prove. But at least it is most likely that the method used in the Alcmaeonid temple had not changed before our earliest references.

It is no doubt a tribute to the predominant fame of Delphi that almost every known form of divination was assigned to it in some ancient author.[1] For instance, Parnassus, the eponymous hero of the mountain, was said to have discovered augury by means of birds, and Delphus and Amphictyon, the heroes of the town and the sacred league invented respectively the examining of entrails and the interpretation of omens and dreams. One body of local priests, the Pyrkooi, were probably concerned with divination by fire and sacrifice. Also the somewhat mysterious nymphs, called the Thriai and connected with Apollo and Parnassus, appear to be personification of the lots used in cleromancy. But in the classical period the fame of Delphi rested on the utterances of the Pythia, who was supposed to speak under the inspiration of Apollo and in his name.

The Pythia rarely figures as an individual in the ancient accounts, because when she spoke, unlike the Sibyl, she was not supposed to be herself consciously uttering an oracle. Her personality was for the time displaced by that of Apollo, and she was merely his medium. Diodorus Siculus (who, as we shall see, recorded a rather rationalistic view of the oracle) stated that originally the Pythia was appointed as a young virgin, but that Echecrates the Thessalian fell in love with the Pythia at a consultation and carried her off and raped her: thereafter the Delphians made a law that no maiden was to act as Pythia, but a woman over fifty who, however, would wear the dress of a maiden in memory of the previous type of prophetess.[2]

This may be taken to be simply an aetiological legend. Classical writers habitually describe the Pythia as old, and the story was invented to explain why she wore the dress of a young girl. The reason was no doubt because of its associations with virgin purity. For the Pythia, as we are told, must be of blameless life, and while she was not disqualified because she had already been a wife and mother, after her appointment she was required to cease to live with her husband, and apparently to observe other restrictive taboos. She had a residence of her own in the sacred enclosure, and evidently led a dedicated life from the time when she took up office. The minimum age of fifty, if it was a rule, was no doubt chosen to assure that she had passed the change in life.

The ritual requirements were clearly determined by the need to ensure the physical purity of the god's instrument. There seems to be no reason to associate them with any belief that the Pythia was the bride of Apollo. Unlike the *promantis* at Patara, she was not shut into the temple itself at night as a preliminary to prophesying, and her age and her dress both indicate that she was not married to the god.

Plutarch and other authors of the second century A.D. go out of their way to emphasise that the Pythia was not selected from any special family nor given a course of particular training. She was a very ordinary peasant woman who had no particular gifts when not inspired by Apollo. How, then, she was selected is never explained, but elsewhere I have called attention to the resemblance between her ritual qualifications and those of the guild of holy women who had the sole

duty of keeping alight the eternal fire inside the temple.[3] It was fed
with supplies of pine and laurel only by women 'who had ceased from
marital relations'. This would presumably involve a number of
attendants working in shifts day and night, and these would provide
a suitable nucleus from whom a Pythia could be selected. Actually in
the heyday of the oracle, as we shall see, there were as many as three
Pythiae at a time: two alternating in actual service, and one held in
reserve. So in the period when the business of the oracle made heavy
demands on the prophetesses, their work could be organised to bear it
and beginners could be trained in, even if they started with no previous
preparation.

(2) METHODS OF INDUCING INSPIRATION

How, then, were these elderly women induced to behave as mediums
and speak with the voice of Apollo? This is a question which is not
asked in the early classical period. As we have seen, Apollo was
associated with mediumistic prophecy in a number of his temples elsewhere in Greece and Asia Minor. His normal mouthpiece was a man,
and the precise ritual preceding the ecstatic utterance varied from place
to place. In Delphi all the early emphasis is on the tripod. This was in
origin an ordinary domestic utensil for cooking: three metal legs supported a bowl which could thus be suspended over a fire so that its
contents could be warmed. But starting from its practical uses in
preparing ritual feasts the tripod became a recognised offering to the
gods even without the intention of putting it to any use. Apollo was
the frequent recipient of such dedications, not only at Delphi, but also
at other shrines, and other gods also received them to an equal extent.
For instance at Dodona excavation has produced the remains of tripods from the eighth century, and there was a remarkable story
describing how ultimately there were so many of them that they could
be arranged in a huge circle touching each other round the sacred oak.[4]

One peculiar use of the tripod by Apollo, perhaps specially at
Delphi, was to occupy it as a throne. Literature and art represent the
god seated in the bowl, and also the Pythia as prophesying is regularly
shown and described in the same position. Why exactly the tripod
should be converted in this way into the seat of the god or of his
human representative is not easy to explain. Perhaps the conception

dates back to a time before cult images were produced as the central object of worship. At such a time a tripod might have become the focal point and the god have been imagined as occupying this place on it. The extreme limits of the development of the idea seem to be between 1000 and 750 B.C. for this is the period of the evolution of the lebes-tripod, which was a type of utensil invented in Greece and not exported. It would suit with what we have already seen of the history of Delphi, if the Pythia first began to seat herself on the tripod towards the end of that period.

If we suppose that the Pythia spoke in a mediumistic trance, the mechanism required was some powerful suggestion which would, as though by hypnotism, temporarily displace her normal personality. For this purpose the act of seating herself in the tripod could well make a fitting climax, especially if it was situated in a place of peculiar reverence, the innermost sanctuary of a temple, and was sincerely believed otherwise to be occupied only by the god himself. The suggestion could also be assisted by other elements of preliminary ritual. Our evidence for these is mostly late and of rather doubtful authority, but the uses of laurels and sacred water are both at least possible.[5] The laurel, as we have seen, was Apollo's tree, and certainly there were laurel branches in his sanctuary which the Pythia is described as shaking. Also from at least the fifth century B.C. there are references to the chewing of the bitter leaves of the laurel by prophets or poets so as to acquire inspiration. But the practice is not actually attributed to the Pythia until the second century A.D. Similarly, the sacred springs of Delphi may have had their ritual purposes. All earlier accounts treat Castalia as the source of water for purification, not for inspiration, and when the idea of inspiration first emerges, it is for poets and not prophetesses. Only in late periods and in rather peculiar ways Castalia is linked with the Pythia's utterances. Within the sacred enclosure itself there was a much smaller spring, Cassotis, of which Pausanias records:

they say that its water plunges underground and in the innermost sanctuary (*adyton*) of the god makes the women prophetic.

This is one point at least on which the excavation of the temple has given decisive evidence. No conduit led into the innermost sanctuary. But curiously enough everything was arranged in such a way as to convey this impression. As J. Pouilloux has lately shown, the water from Cassotis, situated on a higher terrace above the temple, was carried away round its west end by an underground channel without approaching the building. But anyone who has explored the southern side of the temple basement is familiar with a peculiar contrivance of channels which appears to provide for a stream issuing from under the *adyton*. Actually, as was first observed by F. Courby, the water was carried by one conduit to a small reservoir in the inner foundations of the sixth-century temple and then issued again from the wall by a conspicuous channel. But the reservoir had no connection with the inner sanctuary, and water could only have been drawn from it outside the temple basement.

The purpose of the elaborate construction is hard to explain. It is unlikely that it was simply intended to convey the illusion that a sacred spring issued from the *adyton* where it was available to the Pythia. More probably those who contrived the system believed that the basement of the temple was itself a holy place, and that water conveyed to a reservoir in it would emerge charged with some special properties. Certainly the use of the stream for this purpose went back to the construction of the sixth-century temple. But what functions, if any, the water from this source played in the temple ritual cannot now be proved, except that Plutarch referred to it as used for libations and lustrations.

The Pythia may, then, perhaps specially in late periods, have reinforced her inspiration by chewing laurel leaves or drinking sacred water. One other piece of preliminary ritual of a different kind is well evidenced from our sources.[6] Before the Pythia sat on the tripod, the priests had to ascertain whether the god was favourable to a consultation. The method used was to present a goat as an offering, but before it could be sacrificed the victim must give the auspicious omen by trembling from head to foot through all its limbs. To induce this trembling the priests adopted the rather naive device of sprinkling the goat with cold water and repeating the process till either they produced the desired omen or they were satisfied that it was not forthcoming on this occasion. The underlying theory evidently was that the goat should tremble just as the Pythia trembled in ecstasy, and that both conditions were the work of the god. If the goat trembled first, then by analogy the priestess too would tremble. But also in a primitive way, more resembling the equivocations of Roman ritual, the goat needed a physical stimulus before it would do its part.

(3) THE CHASM AND THE VAPOUR

In early times, and before rationalism had developed, it was no doubt sufficient for those who consulted the oracle to believe that the Pythia in order to receive inspiration, need only be ritually pure and must seat herself on the tripod of Apollo on an auspicious day. The god would do the rest. But later periods were not content with a simple explanation of this sort, but required a chain of physical causation. Hence Diodorus Siculus, writing in the time of Julius Caesar, produces a rationalistic account of the oracle which he probably extracted from some Hellenistic author.[7] He both provided a story of the origin of Delphi and also an explanation of its contemporary methods.

When Delphi was still uninhabited, a goatherd, named Coretas, observed that any of his goats which approached a certain chasm (on the site of the inner sanctuary of the later temple) skipped in an astonishing fashion and uttered a different cry from their wont. He came near it and had the same experience as the goats, for he was seized with a prophetic frenzy and foretold the future. His utterances were observed by his neighbours, and when they were confirmed by later fulfilment the place of the chasm became frequented, and was regarded as an oracular shrine of Earth. At first the visitors to the place prophesied to each other, but as many in frenzy leapt down the chasm and disappeared, the local inhabitants chose one of their number, a woman, to act as prophetess for all. For her protection they devised the tripod as a contrivance, mounted on which she could sit above the chasm, and, as one is to understand, this method was maintained unchanged after the temple was built and throughout historic times.

This highly ingenious story was evidently concocted by someone well acquainted with Delphic procedure, who wished to account for it all without recourse to religious explanations. The idea of the goats as the original discoverers of the place was derived from the preliminary ritual which we have just described. The tripod itself was explained away as a safety device. The chasm, however, raises a problem. The French excavations unfortunately found that the western end of the temple had been greatly disturbed so that any detailed reconstruction of that part of the building remains impossible. The condition of the site is probably not merely the result of natural causes such as earthquakes, but is to be assigned to deliberate destruction, probably by Christians immediately after the overthrow of paganism. However, one fact is certain: there can never have been any deep subterranean chasm in the rock at this point. Even if allowance is made for subsequent movements of the earth, such a chasm would have left its traces. Of course it would be impossible to prove that there was no superficial cleft a few feet deep, but nothing more is possible. Similarly it is possible that there might have been a low-roofed crypt beneath the general level of the temple floor. Courby proposed to identify traces of a stairway descending to such a place, but later explorers doubt this interpretation.[8]

Our ancient literary sources give no reliable information. Plutarch, who was the priest of the Pythian Apollo in later life, sometimes uses the verb 'descend' of the Pythia going to prophesy, but any significance that she entered an underground chasm is removed by the fact that the same verb is used by Plutarch and others of the enquirers going to the consultation.[9] Possibly the floor of the inner sanctuary may have been a few feet below the general level of the temple pavement.

Plutarch never refers to a chasm as such, though he evidently knew of the legend of Coretas. He does, however, accept the theory of vapour as the source of inspiration, but in a different way.[10] The unnamed source of Diodorus Siculus appears to have drawn his theory from some well-known examples in Asia Minor and elsewhere where poisonous or intoxicating gas issued from caverns. In Plutarch's earlier treatise (the *de defectu*) on the Pythia he accepted this kind of mechanical source of inspiration and was prepared to use it as an explanation for the decline of the Delphic oracle in recent times. The emission of the vapour must be supposed to have decreased. In his later treatise (*De Pythiae Oraculis*), written probably in old age, and when he had been a priest of Apollo for many years, he tends to give the vapour a more spiritual quality. But even in the earlier treatise he had not spoken of the vapour coming from a hole in the ground. The most positive description which he allows himself is to state that

the building in which they make those consulting the god sit down, not often, nor regularly, but occasionally at intervals is filled with a sweet savour and vapour as though the innermost sanctuary (the *adyton*) were emitting, as from a fountain, the scents of the sweetest and most expensive perfumes.[11]

But Plutarch also recognises the practical difficulty that if the vapour issued generally into the place occupied by the priests and enquirers there was no rational ground why they should not prophesy ecstatically.

So Plutarch had to fall back on the further supposition that the Pythia's own state was a determining factor. If she was attuned to the inspiration, then she would be affected by the vapour: if not, it could not influence her or might cause her harm. The god, who knew when the priestess was in a proper state, signified this by making the goat shiver at cold water.

This theory in its very elaboration and vagueness shows how ill the vapour myth fitted the actual circumstances at Delphi. Yet no doubt Plutarch found it preferable to what would otherwise have been the vulgar notion that Apollo managed in some way to insert himself into the Pythia's body and speak through her mouth. The fact was that the ancient world found it extremely difficult to imagine a spiritual force. Inspiration was pictured as being a material and mechanical operation, however fine and subtle the essential spirit which produced it.

Modern geologists will give no support to the theory of vapour from a chasm. The limestone clefts of Delphi might occasionally produce outrushes of cold air, but it would have no chemical properties capable of intoxicating, and the same would apply to the schist which is the other constituent of the local rocks.[12] Essentially the ancient myth was an attempt to rationalise the phenomenon of the Pythia's prophecies. The only point in which it may have had contact with actuality is that, as we have seen, the Pythia might have been herself the successor of a prophetess who used to enter caves for inspiration. This can never have taken place literally on the site of the classical temple, but the cliffs of Delphi have an abundance of limestone openings which might have provided a setting in earlier times, and the tradition of something of the sort may have come down to the Hellenistic writer (evidently well informed on Delphic ritual) from whom Diodorus derived his description. Later Roman authors, influenced perhaps by the Sibyl's cave at Cumae, adopted this actual picture and instead of making the Pythia sit on a tripod over a chasm, made her enter a cave to encounter the vapour.[13] Either version is equally imaginary. At most it is possible that in the floor of the *adyton* there might have been an opening reaching down to the rock below, but this is a mere conjecture.

Though Plutarch did not mean it exactly in that sense, it was true that it was the Pythia's own state of mind which was the determining factor. We need not doubt that the ecstatic prophecies which she uttered were simply the result of suggestion bringing on a trance. A simple peasant woman was brought up from childhood with the current local belief that once seated on the tripod in the inner sanctuary inspiration would come from Apollo. When at last she was selected as Pythia, her personality would react to the stimulus as it was expected to do. Her own self would be submerged and from her subliminal consciousness would come another personality ready to respond to enquiries. To achieve this effect there would be no need of conscious use of hypnotism on the part of the priests. The whole circumstances of the enquiry would supply the needed suggestion. Also when the ceremony was over, and the Pythia returned to her normal self, she would probably show signs of physical exhaustion and certainly would have no conscious memory of what she had said. This circumstance would act as a final confirmation for the priests and enquirers that it was not the Pythia, but the god himself, who had spoken during the consultation.

(4) THE CEREMONY OF CONSULTATION

It is typical of our ancient sources that none of them gives a straightforward account of what happened when a consultation took place. The procedure was no doubt familiar in classical times to many individuals, whether they had attended as private enquirers or on official embassies, and Greek authors take it that the general lines of the ceremony are known and simply refer, as needed, to details. When these are put together a fairly consistent picture emerges, but it is often not possible to be sure that it is complete or alternatively that all the detailed features occurred at all periods.

Plutarch records that originally the Pythia gave oracles once a year only on the seventh of the Delphic month Bysios which fell in early spring and was supposed to be the birthday of Apollo.[14] Monthly, instead of annual, consultations taking place again on the seventh of the month, were introduced as he states at a late date. Of course to Plutarch the origins of Delphi stretched back into the heroic age and a change could come late in its history and still be before the classical period of Greek history. The tradition which he records is not likely to be fallacious. In fact it is probable that the change from the annual to the monthly consultation took place in the sixth century. As we have seen, one of the typical enquiries in earlier periods was the request for authority for a colony, and as the month Bysios ran roughly from mid-February to mid-March and the traditional sailing season started in late March, the sacred calendar would suit very well with this kind of business. Also it would be conveniently before the campaigning season for military enquirers.

When the establishment of the Amphictyonic control of the sanctuary had given Delphi a basis for still wider business, it is probable that the change was made from annual consultations to occasions when as one of the interlocutors in Plutarch's dialogue says 'the god is shut in a mortal body once a month'.[15] In addition the rule applied that Apollo was absent for the three winter months, and at this period the oracle was closed. So one can take it that consultations by means of the ecstatic prophecies of the Pythia were available on nine days of the year.

Some scholars have felt it was too difficult to accept the clear statements of our ancient sources on this point, because they could not believe that the Delphic priests would be willing to limit their occasions for enquiry in this way. But it is a dangerous *a priori* argument, as we can never tell how strong the belief in some divine restrictions on the operation of the oracle might be. Actually, however, as we shall see the priests could get round the restriction by using other methods of divination. So far as the ecstatic prophecies of the Pythia were concerned, two points significantly reinforce the idea that the occasions of consultation were severely limited.

One of the favourite honours conferred by the Delphians on states or individuals was *promanteia*—the right of precedence in making a consultation.[16] The Delphians themselves claimed the first place, but sometimes they awarded the next place to a favoured city, and more often they assigned what appears to have been a general right of precedence, which presumably gave the recipient a place ahead of all those without this privilege. Similarly individuals could be voted this honour. Of course a preferential rank would in itself confer distinction, but it becomes much more significant if we recognise that the enquiries had to be packed into the space of one day, and if they were not completed then must be postponed for a month.

That this kind of crowded queue of enquirers to be dealt with in one day was a regular feature of the oracle is proved by a remarkable statement of Plutarch.[17] When contrasting contemporary auditions at Delphi with the days when Greece was more populous, he remarks that then

they employed two prophetesses assigned for duty in turn, and a third was appointed as a reserve.

The description indicates that consultations went on throughout the day from dawn to dark with two Pythiae working in shifts, while a third was held in reserve to be called on, if either of the two had to give up. Such a severe pressure of business is only consistent with the view which we have already accepted that the consultations took place on one day only in the month. If they had been possible on most days it is too difficult to explain why there would be such urgency.

The details of procedure, as we have explained, are hard to determine.[18] At dawn or soon after the Pythia purified herself in preparation for the consultation. Our sources refer to her washing herself at Castalia and fumigating herself with laurel leaves and barley meal at the sacred hearth. Then the priests, before declaring the day auspicious and admitting the priestess to the innermost sanctuary, presented the sacrificial goat before Apollo and tested the omens by sprinkling it with cold water. Failure to obtain the proper indication would lead to a cancelling of the enquiries for that day. When the sign had been given the victim was offered, probably on the great altar of the Chians outside the temple, so that all enquirers might know that the day had been found auspicious. The Pythia was then admitted to the sanctuary and may have gone through further preliminaries, such as chewing laurel leaves or drinking sacred water to assist inspiration. Finally she mounted the tripod. In the meantime the male officials of Delphi had also been preparing themselves for the ceremony by a lustration at Castalia. The exact composition of this official body is uncertain and may probably have varied from time to time in the history of Delphi. Different authorities mention the chief of the priests, who was known as the *Prophetes*, his priestly colleagues, the *Hosioi* (a clan devoted to the worship of Dionysus as well as Apollo) and some representatives of the Delphic community selected by lot. The enquirers also had to purify themselves with holy water, and were allowed to consult the oracle in turn, the order being determined partly by precedence and partly by lot.

Before each enquirer was allowed to enter the temple, he must first offer on the altar outside a sacred cake whose cost was fixed at a high price. This procedure in effect served as the minimum charge for consulting the oracle. It would be interesting if we could form a clear picture of the tariff. But, as is typical of so much of our ancient evidence, we do not know the standard prices, but only two special conventions agreed at different periods with the states of Phaselis and Sciathus.[19] Presumably they represented some reduction on the normal rates. About 420 B.C. the Phaselites agreed to pay seven (Aeginetan) drachmae and two obols for a state enquiry and a tenth of that sum for a private individual. This rather clumsy sum was evidently intended to be the equivalent of ten Attic drachmae for a state enquiry. So we can picture that the Phaselite who came personally to consult the oracle would be charged as a minimum one Attic drachma or the equivalent of two days' pay for an Athenian juryman of the time. Some fifty years later the state of Sciathus was to be charged at a far lower rate. It need only pay two (Aeginetan) drachmae and its private enquirers a sixth of that amount. As the cost of living in Greece was rising at the time, it is puzzling to find the Delphic tariff falling so steeply. If business had been declining it might have been necessary to reduce charges, but a more probable explanation is that the small and poor island of Sciathus was recognised by the Delphic authorities as unable to meet a heavy fee and so they may have been let off specially lightly. In each instance, however, we note that the principle is maintained that the payment by a state must be many times that of a single person.

The sacred cake was not the end of the enquirer's expenses. After he had passed the threshold into the cella of the temple, he had still to sacrifice sheep or goats on the inner hearth, where burned the eternal fire. (Throughout the ritual the enquirer was accompanied by the priests and the *proxenus*—the local representative of his city—for these had to guide him through the proper ritual.) It was at this point no doubt that the individual could exhibit his piety and generosity by the amount of the sacrifice offered. In primitive times the Delphians had traditionally snatched for themselves a share of the meat from the victim. The procedure was supposed by legend to date back at least to the time of the Trojan war, when according to one version it had been the occasion for Neoptolemus' death when he resisted the outrageous attempt. Also it was still practised in the sixth century if the story is correct that Aesop earned the Delphians' hate by mocking at the performance. Probably later the local inhabitants were simply assigned a share.

When the sacrifice was ended, the enquirer was admitted to the inner sanctuary reserved for the consultation. This was probably a small building opening off the central court of the temple and at its south-western end. The limits of its dimensions appear to have been some sixteen feet long by nine broad. No woman except the Pythia herself might enter it. The male enquirer was made to seat himself at the nearer end of the room and was warned to 'think pure thoughts and speak well-omened words'. The latter part of this command in effect imposed silence on him. Before he had entered, the Pythia was already under the influence of Apollo and was in some abnormal state of trance. It would appear that neither the enquirer nor even the *Prophetes* could see her. Either the most holy part of the building in which she was seated on the tripod was at a lower level, or more probably it was simply cut off by a curtain from the gaze of those consulting her. The *Prophetes*, who had already received the enquirer's question in verbal or written form, put it to the Pythia, and conveyed the answer back. Whether the enquirer himself could hear distinctly what the Pythia said is never stated, for our authorities draw no distinction between the answer as spoken by her and as conveyed by the *Prophetes*, and yet it is clear that he was responsible for reducing it to form. The references to the Pythia's voice often imply that she did not speak in ordinary tones, but cried or shouted. This circumstance would be quite consistent with a trance state. One may suppose, too, that her replies may have been confused and incoherent. It was the business, then, of the *Prophetes* to make sense from them and to reproduce them in verse. The traditional form was in hexameters, and the oral conventions of the epic had provided a pattern, so that it was not too difficult for him to produce these impromptu.[20]

When the reply had been spoken to the enquirer, the consultation

was over, and the enquirer left the temple. Stories of a dialogue between those consulting and the Pythia are rare and obviously fictitious.
The answer could be recorded in writing for transmission and if the
enquirer was simply an agent it might be given to him sealed. Once it
was delivered verbally or in written form, the Delphic authorities
ceased to concern themselves with it further. They did not provide any
official gloss or interpretation. For that purpose the enquirer might go
to a prophetic expert in his own city or elsewhere, who might claim
to be able to expound the meaning of Apollo's oracles. For, quite
apart from the conventions of the verse form, it was popularly accepted
that the god answered in riddles. In most of the extant verse responses
the god speaks in the first person—only in late and unauthentic
instances the reply is drafted in the third person. For the Pythia was
believed not to be answering out of her own consciousness but in the
person of the god.

(5) THE LOT ORACLE

It is not surprising that when performed with due solemnity of ceremonial in the incomparable setting of the Castalian gorge and Parnassus, the proceeding of consulting the Pythian Apollo had a powerful
effect on the enquirer. Delphi in the mid-sixth century was no doubt
the most famous and successful of the Greek oracle centres and in
spite of difficult times and mistakes in policy was to maintain this position for a couple of centuries. The stream of enquirers wishing to
consult the god must far have exceeded those who could be fitted into
the short space of one day in the month. So though our literary sources
do not make it clear, the priests evidently developed an alternative
method of divination which could be practised much more frequently.
This was by the use of lots, a procedure whose existence at Delphi was
not generally recognised by modern scholars until the inscription was
found which regulated its tariff for the people of Sciathus.[21] This, as
we have seen, was a convention made in the early fourth century B.C.
In it the phrase occurs that if the enquirer 'presents himself for the
[method of] two beans, the charge to the state is an Aeginetan stater'.
This can only mean some process of drawing lots to determine the
answer to an alternative question. It would most likely take the
traditional form: 'is it better and more good that I adopt such and such

a course?' Then a bean of one colour would give a favourable answer and indicate 'yes', while the other bean of a different colour would convey the opposite meaning.

The inscription proves beyond doubt that the method was normal in the fourth century, but probably it began long before that date. Ancient authors only twice describe the Pythia as drawing lots in a formal consultation and in each instance the enquiry called for a selection of names. One example is fully authentic. When Cleisthenes in the last years of the sixth century established the new organisation of the Athenian citizens in ten tribes, the Pythia was asked to select the names of ten heroes from a list of a hundred. These then became the eponyms of the new tribes. The other story is likely to be at best very legendary in its present form. It told how when the Thessalians wished to appoint a king they sent a number of names to the Pythia. Aleuas' father would not let his name be put in, but his uncle inserted it surreptitiously, and the Pythia drew it and subsequently vouched for the selection by a hexameter response. If the story were authentic, it would show that the Pythia was already drawing names in the latter half of the seventh century B.C., and it is not impossible that this method of appointing the federal leader of Thessaly was primitively employed. Homer gives good evidence that it was early believed that the gods guided the drawing of names.[22]

The two instances recorded in literature are both special examples of the Pythia's activity. Evidence that she could draw lots to determine ordinary enquiries is better provided by the verb which is used in both these contexts and often elsewhere in describing the Pythia's action. This is 'to pick up' (*anhairein*) and was the appropriate term to use of lifting a lot out of a container. It is often employed in contexts where it is translated 'the Pythia gave a prophetic response', and evidently it became in Greek prose the usual term to convey this meaning. Its earliest occurrence in this sense appears to be in Thucydides, but he evidently treats it as a normal usage, and it may well have been established with this meaning a couple of centuries before.[23]

The other indication that cleromancy had a primitive connection with Delphi is found in the obscure reference to the Thriae, the nymphs personifying lots.[24] They are described as dwelling on Parnassus and being the nurses of Apollo. The earliest allusion to them in a rather cryptic form occurs in the *Homeric Hymn to Hermes* and probably dates from the sixth century. So from these rather vague literary indications we can carry back the use of lots by the Pythia from the fourth century to the archaic period, and conjecture that it was sometime before 500 B.C. that it became an accepted practice that on other days of the month, when the Pythia did not sit on the tripod, she answered enquiries by drawing lots. These probably were beans coloured black or white to give favourable or unfavourable answers, but also at times they could have names inscribed on them, not only of heroes or candidates for kingship, but also one may suppose of gods to whom the enquirer should sacrifice. For a favourite enquiry would be, 'to what god or hero must I pray or sacrifice to achieve such and such a purpose'.

The comparative silence of our literary authorities suggests that they regarded the use of lots as of less significance and repute than the procedure of ecstatic prophecy. It is obvious that the inspired Pythia on the tripod gave much more scope for picturesque treatment in prose or verse. The Delphic authorities may have been conscious themselves that the method of the lot was somewhat too easy and popular. By the third century B.C. at least there was in circulation an hexameter line attributed to Pythia: 'many are they that throw lots, but few are the men who are prophets'.[25] This presumably was less intended to depreciate the entire use of cleromancy than to suggest that it needed to be employed by a qualified agent.

What the procedure was at Delphi, we are never told. It might be unwise to assume that the ceremony was exactly parallel to ecstatic prophecy. For instance it is never stated that it took place in the innermost sanctuary. There are some obscure references to lots lying in the tripod, but this need mean no more than that there was their usual resting place. It would be suitably chosen to bring them into contact with the god's inspiration. One phrase may suggest that the ceremony of drawing the lots took place in public. Xenophon, when describing through the mouth of Socrates, Chaerephon's famous enquiry about him, says the answer was given 'in the presence of many'.[26] I have argued elsewhere that this consultation was probably made by drawing lots, and no other supposition would explain how Xenophon (who himself had consulted the Delphic oracle on more than one occasion) could make a statement quite inappropriate to a response given in the inner sanctuary. The Pythia may have performed the ceremony in the hypaethral court of the temple or even in the entrance colonnade. At any rate one is led to suppose that while the Pythia's prophecies in ecstasy for ritual reasons were only allowed nine times in the year and were surrounded with elaborate ceremonial, the consultation by lot took place on any day in nine months that was not actually inauspicious, and could be managed with much less trouble and expense. For the private individual it probably became the normal method of enquiry.

NOTES

1. For references, see Parke and Wormell, *Delphic Oracle 1*, 9 ff.
2. Diodorus Siculus, *16*, 26. For the Pythia as old: Aeschylus, *Eumenides*, 38 and Euripides, *Ion*, 1324
3. Parke and Wormell, *1*, 35 with references
4. The tripod and Delphi: Parke and Wormell, *1*, 24 with references. The tripod at Dodona: Stephanus of Byzantium under the caption Dodona
5. For the laurel and the sacred spring, see the discussion in Parke and Wormell, *1*, 26 ff. For the water in the *adyton*: Pausanias, *10*, 24, 7. But see F. Courby, *Fouilles de Delphes*, 2, 181 ff. and J. Pouilloux, *Énigmes à Delphes*, 92 ff.
6. Plutarch, *Moralia*, 3, 435B, 437B and 438A
7. Diodorus Siculus, *16*, 26
8. *Fouilles de Delphes*, 2, 59 ff.
9. 'Descend', of the Pythia: Plu. *3*, 397A, 405C and 438B, Diogenes Laertius, *5*, 6, 91; of enquirers: Pindar, *Pythian Odes* 4, 55, Herodotus, 5, 92, Plu. *3*, 407D and *Timoleon*, 8
10. See R. Flacelière, *Revue des Études Grèques* 56 (1943), 72 ff.
11. Plu. *3*, 437C
12. Philippson, Pauly-Wissowa, 5, col. 2519 and J. Bousquet, *Bulletin de Correspondance Hellénique* 64–65 (1940–1), 228
13. e.g. Livy, *1*, 56, 10, Lucan, *5*, 111 and *6*, 425
14. Plu. *Moralia*, 3, 292E
15. Plu. *Moralia*, 3, 398A
16. See the discussion in P. Amandry, *Mantique*, 113–14
17. Plu. *Moralia*, 3, 414B
18. cf. Parke and Wormell, *1*, 30 ff. with references
19. Phaselis: Schwyzer, *Dialectorum Graecorum Exampla*, 332; Sciathus: *BCH*. 63 (1939) 184 ff., and 68–9 (1944–45), 411 ff. For a general discussion: Amandry, *Mantique*, 86 ff.
20. cf. Wallace E. McLeod. Oral Bards at Delphi. (*Transactions and Proceedings of the American Philological Association*) 92 (1961), 317
21. See note 19

22. Cleisthenes: Parke and Wormell, *2*, no. 80. Aleuas: id, no. 316. On the gods directing lots, Hom. *Il. 8*, 175 ff.
23. Thucydides, *1*, 118, 3
24. Parke and Wormell, *1*, 10 and note 23
25. Zenobius, *5*, 75
26. Xenophon, *Apology*, 14; *Classical Philology*, 56 (1961), 249

8

DELPHI'S RIVALS

(1) DODONA

After following the growth of Delphi's importance for two centuries it is time to consider more briefly some of the rival institutions over which it was achieving a lead. Dodona, as we saw, had probably long preceded Delphi as a place of consultation, since it dated back into the Mycenaean age. In the archaic period when Delphi was acquiring its pre-eminence, it had forced its way into some of the legends previously associated with Dodona. But one passage in Greek literature survives in fragmentary form where the claims of Dodona are strongly pressed. It is a quotation from the lost Hesiodic poem, the *Eoiai*:

There is a certain Hellopia of much cornland and good meadow rich in flocks and shambling cattle, and in it dwell men of many sheep and many kine, many themselves in number, past telling, tribes of mortals. There a certain Dodona is built as a town at the farthest bound. It Zeus has loved and [wished it] to be his oracle-centre for mankind [just at this most interesting point the citation seems to have suffered from a lacuna. It continues:—] And they dwelt in the stem of the oak where those who live on earth fetch all their prophecies, whoever of them has come thither and enquired of the immortal god bringing gifts when he came and accompanied by good omens.[1]

This passage is very different in tone from the allusions to Dodona in Homer. The place is not inclement, but prosperous. The fact that Zeus loves it and has chosen it as his oracle contains a covert blow at Delphi. The reference in the lacuna was probably to the doves associated with the oracle. The oak itself is not explained, but some account of it also was probably contained in the lacuna. So this Hesiodic fragment which clearly refers to the oracle as a contemporary institution is evidence for the functioning of Dodona in the late eighth or seventh century much as in the period before the Dark Ages. This is confirmed also by the excavation of the site. From the mid-eighth century at least a succession of bronze objects—fragments of tripods, fibulae and so forth—were found, which, though uninscribed at this date, are best explained as dedications given by grateful enquirers. They are the first of a series which continues down the classical period.[2]

Dodona was evidently functioning as an oracle throughout this time, but our literary references give us no clue to its procedure till Herodotus visited it about the forties of the fifth century.[3] Then he suggests a very different picture of the organisation from what we get in Homer. The Selli are not mentioned: in their place are three priestesses, whose names he gives. The sacred oak and the doves are not treated as a means of consulting the god. They only figure in legend connected with the founding of the oracle. This foundation itself is extraordinarily linked with the oracle of Ammon in Libya, so as to suggest that they were both sister colonies from Egyptian Thebes, and finally on the method of divination employed Herodotus simply remarks that it is the same in Dodona as in Egypt.

Clearly a complete transformation had come over the oracle of Dodona. Later Classical authors comment on the fact, and Strabo explains it by connecting the appointment of priestesses with the introduction of the worship of Dione, the consort of Zeus.[4] But this is a very improbable conjecture. Dione by her name and all other indications was not an independent deity invading Dodona from abroad, but was simply a female counterpart of Zeus, from whom her name derives. She is regularly grouped with him, but in a subordinate position, in enquiries addressed to the oracle, and Herodotus who gives our earliest and best evidence on the priestesses never mentions her at all.

The more probable explanation is that the authorities of Dodona were imitating Delphi. There, as we have seen, in the heyday of the oracle its replies were conveyed by three Pythiae. Also Herodotus' reference to the method of divination points in the same direction. By treating it as similar to that of Egypt, he implies some form of written enquiry which received a 'yes' or 'no' answer from the god. This is exactly what the archaeological finds at Dodona indicate.

There have been recovered at various places in the sacred precincts the remains of numerous thin strips of lead on which had been scratched written questions addressed to Zeus.[5] These tablets were evidently supplied by the authorities to each enquirer who wrote the question himself. It was then folded so that the writing was hidden and a number or an abbreviated name or some similar indication was incised on the outside so that it could be identified without being unfolded. From one reference to lots and a jar in connection with the oracle and a number of artistic representations of priestesses in action one can conjecture that the written question was put into some vessel with a narrow neck from which the priestess extracted it and probably at the same time drew out a bean or some other symbol which showed whether the god's reply was favourable or unfavourable. The thin lead tablets were evidently folded for two purposes. The small size made it possible to insert them and extract them from a jar, and the priestess could not read the contents of the enquiry when she gave the god's decision on the question which it asked.

The system was already established some time before Herodotus visited Dodona, and the fact is confirmed by the sequence of lead tablets which appear to start about the end of the sixth or beginning of the fifth century. Taken in conjunction with the remains of dedications from the site, they indicate a thriving business. The lead tablets were apparently retained by the authorities after the enquiry and often were unfolded and smoothed for use again by subsequent enquirers. Consequently a large number of them are palimpsests with traces of several previous questions. The large majority of the enquirers are private individuals. None of the consultations by states as evidenced dates before the last quarter of the fifth century. But this may be a mere accident in the examples preserved. However, the general impression from the forms of dialect and writing is that the enquirers were mostly from west Greece and the Peloponnese.

While a major factor in determining the changes at Dodona from the Selli and the oak to the priestesses and a lot-oracle may have been conscious imitation of Delphi, there also may have been another factor which might have forced on the authorities the need for a change. This was the oak-tree itself. If we picture as we should that there had been a single tree which was the sacred oak of Zeus and which had been the object of cult and the source of enquiry since before 1200 B.C. at least, there is still the problem of its survival. Oaks have a famous reputation for longevity, but even so, much more than five hundred years would be highly exceptional and, while it is impossible to draw a rigid line, seven or eight hundred years can be taken as the ultimate limit. So an oak which was venerable enough to be a mere century old at the time of the Trojan war would be in the last stages of decrepitude by the sixth century B.C. The disposition of the buildings in the sanctuary at Dodona suggests that in the fourth and third centuries B.C. a space was still left for a sacred tree in a most prominent position,[6] and one can suppose that when the original oak began to die, the priests set about replacing it by another. But even so there may have been an awkward transitional stage, and this may have been the time when the method of the lot-oracle was conveniently introduced. We have no evidence on the subject, but it would not have been beyond the ingenuity of the priesthood to have linked the ceremony of drawing lots with the sacred tree. For instance the affirmative and negative answers and the names of gods and heroes to be drawn might have been written on slips of oak carved from it. Such wooden *sortes* were used in Praeneste. But once the change was introduced, no doubt the method of cleromancy was found much more convenient for dealing with numbers of enquirers.[7]

There is no dependable evidence that the priestesses of Dodona ever attempted to imitate the Pythiae in ecstatic prophecy. Plato once refers to the two groups of prophetesses together as though they both were inspired with a divine madness, but this is probably a mistake on his part. Also in Hellenistic times Dodona had circulated verses said to have been produced by the Peleiades (their first priestesses) before Phemonoe, the traditional first Pythia.[8] But this is only another instance of the rivalry in publicity between these two oracles.

(2) OTHER APOLLINE ORACLES

If we look round the other instances of Delphi's rivals at the time of the Persian conquest of Asia Minor, there was probably no serious competitor in the Peloponnese. Olympia, a centre of the cult of Zeus since the Dark Ages, had an oracle in early times, but by the sixth century with the growing dominance of the Olympic games it was specialising in foretelling the chances of success of the competitors by the omens to be derived from sacrifices.[9]

Much nearer to Delphi there were at least four Apolline oracles: at Abae in Phocis, and in Boeotia at Tegyra and on Mount Ptoion and of the Ismenian Apollo at Thebes. Neither Abae nor Tegyra have been excavated, and our literary sources give virtually no picture of their activity. One may conjecture that Abae tended to be treated as a national centre by the Phocians, especially after the Amphictyonic league controlled Delphi. The Ptoion sanctuary appears from the French excavations to have been the cult-centre of a mother-goddess and a hero (Ptoios) until under Theban influence about 600 B.C. Apollo came in and took over the chief place. The medium, as we have seen, was a prophet speaking in ecstasy. There is no evidence to suggest that he sat on a tripod, but tripods were a favourite form of dedication in accordance with the god's instructions. The Ismenian Apollo at Thebes, as Herodotus records, was consulted by sacrifices as at Olympia. Also there were two sanctuaries of heroes, Amphiaraus and Trophonius, which were in regular use. In each instance it seems that the deity was really a god of the underworld, whose primitive cult had tended to be reduced in status compared with the Olympians. Amphiaraus was consulted by dream-oracles and Trophonius had a peculiar ritual whereby the enquirer entered a hole in the ground and himself produced his own prophecy by the confused remarks which he made on emerging. Our detailed account of the oracle dates from the second century A.D., but literary references show that it was already operating by the sixth century B.C. Probably most of these centres had only local importance, but the Ptoion and the shrine of Trophonius were of rather wider appeal.[10]

In the Cyclades Delos had once had an Apolline oracle of importance. This fact can be seen from the *Homeric Hymn to Apollo*, where the island exacts from Leto an oath that the god when born will make on it his first temple to be an oracle-centre for men. One can suppose that this institution existed at the time when this part of the hymn was composed, probably at the end of the eighth century, and may have dwindled away in the seventh century when presumably the original Ionian festival which the poet described died out. By the time when Pisistratus and Polycrates in the latter half of the sixth century revived the sanctity of Delos, the oracle appears to have already ceased and was not restored. There is no sign that at this time the Delian priesthood were linked in any way with Delphi. In fact at some time

before the mid-fifth century they developed instead a peculiar association with Dodona in connection with the Hyperborean gifts.[11]

On Asia Minor Didyma near Miletus is the only oracle-centre for
whose activity we have some evidence in the sixth century. There
were no doubt already established temples of Apollo also at Gryneum
and Claros, where from the Hellenistic period famous sources of responses flourished. But though our literary authorities show that they
had existed from the archaic period at least, there is no reference to
any enquiries made there. Like so much of the history of Ionia it seems
to have been swallowed up by the Persian conquest. But Herodotus
preserves one interesting story about the oracle of Apollo at Didyma.[12]

Pactyes, a Lydian, who had led a national revolt against Cyrus soon
after the fall of Sardis, when his attempt had failed, took refuge in
Cyme. The Persians sent to demand his surrender, and the men of
Cyme dispatched a sacred embassy to ask the oracle what they should
do about Pactyes so as to please the gods. The reply came that they
should hand him over to the Persians and the Cymeans were prepared
to act accordingly, but an opposition was led by one Aristodicus who
persuaded them not to do so because he doubted the response and did
not believe that the embassy had given a true report. Accordingly a
second group of ambassadors including Aristodicus were sent and
asked the same question, but emphasised that Pactyes was a suppliant.
The god once more commanded them to surrender him. Aristodicus,
however, was still not content, but proceeded to go round the temple
pulling down the nests of the sparrows and other birds which had
settled in the building. While he was doing this, as the story went, a
voice, evidently supernatural, came from the innermost sanctuary
crying: 'most wicked man, why do you dare to act thus: to ravage the
suppliants from the temple', to which Aristodicus unabashed replied,
'O lord, do you yourself thus rescue your suppliants, while you bid
the men of Cyme to surrender their suppliant'. But the god had the
last word. For he answered, 'Yes, I bid them, in order that they may
commit impiety and come to speedier destruction, so that in future
you will not approach an oracle with a question about surrendering
suppliants.' The Cymeans might well be puzzled by this response, and
actually they achieved a compromise by sending Pactyes away to
another Greek city.

NOTES

1. Hesiod, *Fr.* 134
2. Parke, *Oracles of Zeus*, 99 ff. with references
3. Herodotus, 2, 52 ff.
4. Strabo, *7*, 7, 12 and for a more detailed discussion, *Oracles of Zeus*, 69 ff.
5. *Oracles of Zeus*, 100 ff. and 259 ff. (appendix 1)
6. S. I. Dakaris, 'Das Taubenoakel von Dodona' *Antike Kunst*, 1963, 35–49
7. Cicero, *De Div.* 2, 85
8. Plato, *Phaedrus*, 244B. The Peliades: Pausanias, *10*, 12, 10
9. *Oracles of Zeus*, 183 ff.
10. e.g. Herodotus, *8*, 133, and *1*, 49 (Amphiaraus)
11. *Homeric Hymn.* cf. supra p. 38. Delos and Dodona: e.g. Herodotus, *4*, 32
12. Claros: *Homeric Hymn*, 9, 4, Gryneum; Strabo, *13*, 3, 5, Didyma: Herodotus, *1*, 46

9

DELPHI IN THE INTERNATIONAL CRISIS

The story of Pactyes the Lydian has obviously been worked up into a pious legend, but no doubt it was founded on fact. We may suppose that the Branchidae, the priests of Apollo of Didyma, had recommended the surrender of Pactyes. It was only one instance of a problem which in various forms was to puzzle the prophets of Ionia and mainland Greece. Were they to counsel appeasement of Persia or were they to encourage action against her at whatever risk? We can imagine that the question must have struck home particularly severely to the authorities of Delphi. They had received unparalleled bounty from the kings of Lydia and had no doubt replied with encouraging responses. Now Lydia was destroyed; their confidence in its strength had proved utterly mistaken; what could they suppose except that Persia was invincible and any attempt at resistance futile?

The new policy of submission to Persia is illustrated by an enquiry from the people of Cnidus with Apollo's reply, preserved by a local tradition.[1] The Cnidians had originally decided to resist the invaders and were proceeding to cut a canal through the isthmus which connected their peninsula with Asia Minor, but the workmen suffered a phenomenal number of casualties through the splintering of the rock. So evidently regarding this as a sign of supernatural disapproval, they sent to Delphi to ask for an explanation. The response contained a direct prohibition—

'. . . But as for the isthmus, neither fortify it nor dig it. For Zeus would have made it an island, if he had wished it so.'

D

The Cnidians therefore abandoned the attempt at fortification.

For the time being the question of resistance to Persia could be left in abeyance. Meantime the Delphians must have been much pre-occupied in the latter half of the sixth century with the rebuilding of the temple after the fire. It was a period of general support of the sanctuary. Beautiful and expensive buildings such as the treasury of the Siphnians were being erected and the precinct was beginning to assume its classical shape with terraces and a rectangular circuit wall. But as late as 515 B.C. the work on the temple itself was still uncompleted. By this date the contract had been taken over by the Alcmaeonidae, a leading family of Athenian aristocrats.[2] They had traditionally been associated with Delphi ever since the First Sacred War, and as leaders of one of the three chief parties in Athens they had alternately opposed and supported the tyrant, Pisistratus. Finally after a temporary recon-ciliation with his sons they had been driven into exile for a second time. Attempts to win back their power by an attack across the Attic frontier had failed. So they had recourse to the oracle as a means of winning a powerful ally. Later the Athenians were prepared cynically to believe that the Pythia had actually been bribed, but there is no need to suppose that the Alcmaeonidae did more than use the influence of their favourable position at Delphi. Anyway the Pythia, as we are told, whenever an enquiry came from the Spartan state or a Spartan indivi-dual included in her response the instruction that they must first free Athens. Pisistratus and his sons had conspicuously avoided any favour-able associations with Delphi and the authorities there would no doubt have been glad to see their friends restored to power. Also Cleomenes, the energetic young king of Sparta, was glad enough to have an excuse for intervention. So in 510 B.C. Hippias the tyrant was expelled from Athens by the Spartans and the Alcmaeonidae were free to return. It was only after an internal struggle and a quarrel with their ally, Cleo-menes, that the family led by Cleisthenes established themselves as leaders of Athens and founders of the democracy. The Pythia was asked to co-operate in the political changes by selecting the names of the ten new tribes into which the citizens were organised.

The Alcmaeonidae witnessed to their gratitude to Apollo by com-pleting his temple with a marble pediment in front instead of the lime-stone one specified in the contract. The building itself was more than a great shrine to house the image of Apollo and be the centre of his worship. It also exhibited, probably for the first time, a prominent statement of the wisdom which he represented. Over the three entrances of the temple were inscribed three aphorisms: 'know thyself', 'nothing too much' and 'go bail and destruction is nigh'.³ Popular tradition later believed that these maxims had been dedicated by the Seven Wise Men who lived at the beginning of the sixth century. If the story was true, they must have made their offering of wisdom to the earlier temple. But the legends about this group of Seven Wise Men date from late in the fifth century and were a subsequent creation while the inscriptions themselves were probably produced for the first time when the Alcmaeonid temple was built.

Of the three, the cautious warning against going bail is rarely quoted, but the other two maxims are constantly cited or referred to in later Greek thought. Occasionally, instead of attributing the origin of their advice to the Wise Men, they were treated as utterances of the Pythian Apollo himself addressed to individual sages. Anyway antiquity agreed in seeing in 'know thyself' and 'nothing too much' the typical expressions of the wisdom of the god. Modern scholars have sometimes been critical of these sentences as expressing too cautious and negative a view of life. But for the ancient Greek they were salutary warnings. To him generally his rather humanised deities were not inclined to suggest the lowly position of man or the need for restraint in his actions. Yet these are the teaching of the Pythian Apollo. The oracle had developed in moral stature. In the seventh century it had stressed blood-guilt and ritual purification; in the sixth it was going further into the question of the individual responsibility and the consciousness of one's limitations.

This development is illustrated by a story in Herodotus, which should date back to the mid-sixth century. A Spartan of high reputation for his uprightness, Glaucus the son of Epicydes, had been entrusted with a large sum of money by a stranger from Miletus. Long after the Milesian's sons arrived to reclaim the deposit, but Glaucus denied that he had ever received the trust, and when challenged to substantiate this by an oath, he consulted Delphi whether he might foreswear himself for the gain which would result. The Pythia gave an utterly uncompromising answer:

'Glaucus, son of Epicydes, for the moment the gain is more thus to conquer with an oath and plunder the money. Swear then, for death awaits even the man whose oaths are true. But the child of an oath has no name and it has no hands or feet. Yet it is swift to pursue until it seize a whole family together and all the house. But the family of the man whose oaths are true is better hereafter.'[4]

If we take the story simply on the basis of the oracular response, it shows a firm, though not surprising, moral tone. But the ending of the story as told by Herodotus carries the point even further. Glaucus, shocked at the Pythia's words, begged forgiveness, but she was not mollified, but told him that to tempt the god and commit the deed were equally heinous. This judgment goes much further than merely maintaining the sanctity of oaths, which the priests could not have failed to do. It raises the whole question of guilt as being a matter of moral intent, rather than overt action. Hendess may have been right in suggesting that it was an accretion to the original story. It is recorded that the Pythia's words were literally fulfilled in that the family of Glaucus did die out. It may have been the need to explain and justify this consequence when he had not actually forsworn himself, which forced the Delphic priesthood to gloss the original story with this additional detail. But even so it indicates the recognition by the Pythian oracle that guilt was a matter of intention, not only of act, and this was a great advance in Greek thought.

While the Delphic oracle's authority in the sphere of morals was extending, in that of politics it became involved in increasing difficulties. At Athens the Alcmaeonidae after a period of dominance fell from power. In Sparta King Cleomenes who had quarrelled with Athens took a vigorous line of policy which raised difficult questions for Delphi. In 494 B.C. he prepared to invade Argos. Both sides consulted the oracle.[5] To Cleomenes the Pythia is alleged to have foretold that he would take Argos. When though victorious he actually failed to do this, a method was found to explain away the prophecy. To the Argives the Pythia gave a much more ambiguous answer which could, however, if necessary have been interpreted in their favour. The more significant circumstance is that the Delphic authorities inserted in the reply a gratuitous and quite irrelevant forecast of the fall of Miletus. In 499 the Ionians had rebelled against Persia, but after some initial success in 494 the fate of Miletus was evidently sealed by the enemy's blockade. The voice of the Pythian Apollo said,

'And then indeed, Miletus deviser of wicked deeds, you will become a feast and bright gifts to many, and your wives will wash the feet of many long-haired men, and others at Didyma will care for our temple.'

The style contains the conventionally figurative usages of Greek oracles, but its meaning is essentially unambiguous, though not directly expressed. Miletus is roundly condemned for its initiative in the revolt and its sack and enslavement are foretold. Evidently Delphi continued in its attitude of appeasement towards Persia. Whether in this policy it was also supported by the oracle of the Branchidae is left vague. Actually the temple shared in the ravaging of Miletus and the oracle—one of Delphi's greatest rivals—was suppressed. The prospect of such an outcome is cautiously suggested in the last line of the prophecy. Later periods were to amplify the story.

Cleomenes sought Delphi's support again a few years later in 491 B.C. His violent policies had involved him in bitter struggles within Sparta, particularly with the king of the other house, Demaratus. To rid himself of his rival he took advantage of an ancient Spartan custom whereby once every eight years the Ephors observed the sky for meteors.[6] The occurrence of a particular sign in the heavens could be taken as an indication that the gods were offended with the kings, and the question must be referred to an oracle for decision. It had often been believed that Demaratus was a bastard. Now Cleomenes contrived to have the question referred to Delphi whether he was legitimate, and working through a Delphian of great influence called Cobon, he persuaded the Pythia Perialla to reply that Demaratus was not the son of King Ariston. For the moment the plot succeeded, Demaratus was deposed, and after lingering a short while in Sparta subject to the insults of his triumphant enemies he fled to Persia. But soon the truth of Cleomenes' conspiring leaked out. Cobon was exiled, Perialla removed from her post, and Cleomenes himself found it expedient to leave Sparta for a time.

This shocking scandal might well have been expected to shake the credit of the Delphic oracle, and it may have roused doubts in some minds. But the fact that the guilty Delphians were punished and that Cleomenes shortly afterwards perished miserably will have satisfied many that the gods exacted due vengeance on wrongdoers. Pausanias looking back on Delphic history more than six hundred years later could regard the crime of Cleomenes as unique.

Much more serious for the attitude of the Greeks to Delphi was the question of resistance to Persia. This reached a critical point with Xerxes' invasion of 480 B.C. Delphi, as we have seen, had already shown itself in favour of appeasement. It had advised the Cnidians against resistance, and had rebuked the Milesian for the Ionic revolt. In face of the Persian king's colossal expedition it advised neutrality to individual states who were as yet uncommitted. When the Argives enquired what was their best policy they were told:

'Foe to those that dwell around you, friend to the immortal gods, stay on guard, keeping your spearpoint within and guard your head. Your head will save your body.'[7]

The Cretans when invited to join the Greek side also consulted Apollo and were scornfully told with mythological examples, that they had had enough troubles already by interfering in other people's quarrels. So they took the advice and remained neutral.[8]

Athens, of course, was in an entirely different position: her support of the Ionic revolt had originally embroiled her with Persia and the victory of Marathon was her great achievement, but it meant that vengeance on Athens was one of Xerxes' chief motives. However, the Athenians consulted the Delphic oracle at some moment shortly before the Battle of Thermopylae. The exact form of the enquiry is not recorded, but must have been on the best course of action in face of the Persian attack. The account of the consultation, as given by Herodotus, is one of the most detailed and circumstantial preserved to us.[9]

After performing the customary rites about the temple, when the ambassadors had entered the hall and sat down, the Pythia whose name was Aristonice, uttered the following oracle:
'Miserable men, why are you sitting idle? Leave in flight the furthest dwellings of your land and the high peaks of the wheel-shaped town. For neither head nor body remains firm, nor tipmost toes nor hands; nor is anything of the middle left, but it is reduced to oblivion. It falls in ruin before fire and sharp Ares, driving a Syrian-born chariot. Many other fortresses he will destroy, not yours alone, and many temples of the immortals he will give to devouring fire, who now stand flowing with sweat, shaking with fear. Down on their topmost roofs black blood has been poured, foreseeing the compulsions of distress. But leave the shrine, ye two, and spread out your hearts to troubles.'

The two ambassadors when they heard these words regarded the situation as very serious. They well might, for the colourful and vehe

ment metaphors of the response left no scope for alternative interpretations. It clearly and unequivocally advised the Athenians to
abandon Attica and flee abroad, as some Ionian cities, such as Phocaea,
had done in face of the original Persian invasion of Asia Minor. The
phrase with which Herodotus introduces the oracle seems to indicate
that on this occasion there had occurred what was often pictured in
legendary examples; the Pythia had not waited for the question to be
formally put to her, but had at once warned the Athenians to rise and
flee. One can only suppose that the line of the reply had already been
fixed by the Delphic authorities, and they had arranged how to put it
over effectively.

The Athenian ambassadors, when they had left the sanctuary,
stopped to debate their next step. No doubt they saw that to return
to Athens with this oracular response would create a furore. The state
had long decided on resistance and would not be prepared to reverse
its policy at a moment's notice. Then, as Herodotus tells the story,
while the ambassadors were deliberating one of the most prominent
Delphians, Timon, the son of Aristobulus, advised them to equip
themselves as suppliants and enter the sanctuary for a second consultation. The Athenians did so and addressed the god:

'O, lord Apollo, utter some better oracle about our native land and pay
respect to these symbols of supplication which we bring, or else we shall
not depart from the innermost sanctuary but shall remain here till we die'.

In answer to this appeal the Pythia uttered a second response:

'Pallas is unable to appease Olympian Zeus, though she prays him with
many words and deep wisdom. But to you again I shall say this which I
have made unshakable as adamant. When all the rest has been captured
which the guardian of Cecrops and the heart of sacred Cithaeron hold between them, yet Zeus of the broad heaven gives to the Tritoborn a wooden
wall, alone to remain undestroyed, and it will bless you and your children.
Do not wait quietly for the cavalry and the mighty host of infantry coming
from the mainland, but turn your back and retire. At some other time you
will yet also stand face to face with them. O divine Salamis, you will destroy
the sons of women either when Demeter is being scattered or when she is
coming together.'

The Athenian embassy could do no better than accept this second
version and return with it to Athens.

The whole episode is highly remarkable for its detail. The responses alone are much longer than those usually quoted for the archaic period. This is probably because elsewhere our ordinary versions do not give the oracular reply *in extenso*, but simply quote from oral tradition the key passage. Also the double consultation is highly exceptional, but can be accepted as fully authentic, not merely because of such details as the name of the Pythia and the name of Timon, but also because no one after the event would have been likely to invent such peculiar happenings and those so little to the credit of the Delphic authorities. Evidently they had decided originally to try to force on the Athenian embassy a command from Apollo that Attica must be abandoned. When the ambassadors were not prepared to return with this response, the Delphic authority thought again. Perhaps there was a strong minority at Delphi who felt that Greek resistance must not be completely discouraged. Evidently there were conversations behind the scenes. Timon appears to be the leader of the Delphians who sympathised with the Athenian point of view and it may have been through him that a hint was conveyed to the priests that if, as seemed likely, resistance by land north of the Isthmus failed, the Athenians would evacuate their population to Salamis and fight in defence of it. The decree of Themistocles now shown on the inscription from Troezen, even if it is not accepted as fully authentic could still be taken to support the view that the Athenian had laid these plans well in advance. Some scholars have regarded the last two lines of the oracle as a *post eventum* addition. But this hypothesis is not necessary. It is interesting instead to notice how the first response, framed with an obvious purpose, is almost without ambiguity. The second response with its metaphor of the wooden wall and its vague allusion to death at Salamis in harvest- or seed-time could fit a naval battle there whatever its date or outcome. The Delphic authorities had given the ambassadors the barest minimum—some authority which Themistocles could interpret as justifying evacuation to Salamis—but had left themselves free to reinterpret the oracle whatever the outcome.[10]

Other oracular responses also were attributed to the Pythia in connection with the events of 480 B.C. The Delphians themselves were said to have consulted Apollo in fear for themselves and the Greeks, and to have received a command to pray to the winds who would be great allies of Hellas. It was a rather obvious suggestion in face of the Persian fleet, and the storms at the time of the battle of Artemisium seemed to fulfil the prophecy. Also the Spartans were quoted as having received a response which indicated either Sparta would be taken or else a Spartan king must fall. This is obviously a *post eventum* prophecy of the death of Leonidas, even containing a figurative play on his name. It was probably produced in the winter of 480–79 with the assistance of the Delphic authorities and with the purpose of inspiriting the Spartans to meet the Persians in the field again by suggesting that the death of Leonidas was a voluntary sacrifice to save his city.[11]

But in the interval between the battle of Thermopylae and the victory of Plataea for some twelve months Delphi lay virtually under Persian control behind their right flank. It would appear that Xerxes made no serious attempt to occupy Delphi. He must have known that its policy was not unfavourable to his side and probably decided that it would prejudice his cause in the eyes of all Greeks if he laid sacreligious hands on the sanctuary of the Pythian Apollo. Later the Delphians told a picturesque legend how a Persian force had tried to force its way there, but had been defeated and destroyed by human defenders and various miraculous happenings. If there was any foundation to the story it probably lay in the unofficial attempt of some unauthorised marauders. From a rather different angle we find the Delphians protecting themselves by fabricating oracles calculated to warn the Persians of the dangers of attacking the temple. By the summer of 479 they may already have been becoming increasingly confident in a victory for the Greek cause and have supplied the Athenians with a forecast for a land victory over the Persians. It was originally drafted so as to suit the plain of Eleusis, but was changed without difficulty by reinterpretation to fit Plataea.[12] Meanwhile the Persians had been attempting to collect their own oracular support from Greek sources.[13] Mardonius when wintering in Thessaly after Salamis sent a Lycian agent named Mys to consult Trophonius at Lebadeia, Abae in Phocis, the Ismenian Apollo at Thebes and Amphiaraus (probably at a shrine in the neighbourhood) and also Apollo at the Ptoion sanctuary. The Boeotian oracle-centres might all be regarded as favourable to the Persian cause at the time. The Phocian priests could not be expected to feel similarly, for as Herodotus records their temple had been sacked in the previous year by the Persian army. Delphi was apparently not consulted whether from deliberate choice or because this was during the winter months of Apollo's absence. Herodotus who had detailed

D*

account of Mys' tour of enquiry neither knew the question which he asked nor the replies which he received. He conjectured plausibly enough that Mardonius was enquiring about his immediate situation and deduced that the answers which he received included advice to win over the Athenians, because the return of Mys to Thessaly was immediately followed by the dispatch of Alexander of Macedon on a diplomatic mission to Athens. Mardonius may have hoped to extract from the oracular responses some useful material for propaganda against the Greek resistance. But the failure of it to be used in this way suggests that he secured nothing significant.

NOTES

1. Herodotus, *1*, 174, 4
2. Herodotus, *5*, 62, 2 ff. and Philochorus (*F. Gr. Hist* 628 f. 115) with Jacoby's detailed commentary. The archaeological evidence for the completion of the temple turns largely on the question of dating the remains of the pedimental sculptures, on which, see Humphry Paine, *Archaic Marble Sculpture from the Acropolis*, pp. 63–4 and 68; De la Coste–Messelière, *Au Musée de Delphes*, p. 82
3. Parke and Wormell, *Delphic Oracle*, *1*, 387 with references
4. Herodotus, *6*, 86
5. The Spartans: Herodotus, *6*, 76, 1, and 80. The Argives: id, 6, 18, and 77, 2
6. Herodotus, *6*, 66 and Parke, *Classical Quarterly* 39 (1945), pp. 100 ff.
7. Herodotus, *7*, 148
8. Herodotus, *7*, 169
9. Herodotus, *7*, 140 ff.
10. For a somewhat different interpretation, see C. Hignett, *Xerxes' Invasion of Greece* (1963), appendix XIII, pp. 439 ff.
11. The Delphians: Herodotus, *7*, 178. The Spartans: id, *7*, 220, 3. For the play on Leonidas' name, cf. Parke and Wormell, *Cl. Qu.* 43 (1949), 139
12. Oracles probably forged in defence of Delphi, Parke and Wormell, *2*, no. 98 and 99. The response before Plataea: id, no. 102
13. Herodotus, *8*, 133

THE ORACLES IN THE CLASSICAL PERIOD

When the Persian wars ended in a complete Greek victory, the Delphic authorities succeeded in re-establishing their position as the spiritual centre of Greece. The oracle had in effect changed sides during the winter of 480–79 and emerged at the time of Plataea as a supporter of the Hellenic cause. Hence when the Persians retreated from Greece and their opponents again took over control of the Delphic Amphictyony, the Pythian Apollo became the recipient of many impressive dedications in honour of the victory. The chief offering of the Greeks as a body took the form of a golden tripod supported by a bronze column formed from three twisted snakes. The Aeginetans gave as their offering the award which they had won for their outstanding bravery at Salamis, a bronze mast surmounted by three golden stars, and other states and individuals were suitably commemorated in the sanctuary.[1]

So for the next fifty years the oracle was able to resume its activity in a manner similar to that of the past. The questions submitted and the answers given seem to have been much on the traditional lines. For instance when the Athenians seized Scyros they received oracular authority to transfer the bones of the Athenian hero, Theseus, from their resting place on the island to a shrine in the Agora. This seems to have served to transfer also some spiritual authority over Scyros, as when the bones of Orestes had been transferred from Tegea to Sparta. Apart from this instance, the Pythia in this period was credited with the establishment of a number of new cults of heroes, who, remarkably enough, were deceased athletes of distinction.[2]

Again when the Athenians founded the colony of Thurii in south

Italy, they were directed by a response of the Pythia in hexameter verse. It may have been delivered earlier to the refugees from Sybaris. Anyway the ambiguities of its description of the site were supplied with a metaphorical interpretation in the best traditional manner.[3] The treasuries and groups of statuary erected at Delphi during the period show that Apollo's prestige continued unshaken. In fact a new tendency shows itself. Evidently it was felt that the control of the oracle was a political asset. So in the struggle for power that developed between Athens and Sparta, Delphi became one of the pieces in the game. It had lain outside the Athenian sphere of influence until the battle of Oenophyta when as a result of the predominance which the Athenians acquired over Boeotia, Delphi fell into the control of the Phocians, who were their allies. The Spartans managed once to intervene by force of arms and restore the Delphians to their previous independence. But Pericles immediately afterwards reversed the position which remained to Athens' advantage until the battle of Coronea broke their hold on western Boeotia.

It may have been during this period of her dominance at Delphi that Athens was addressed by the Pythia in the verses which were often quoted later when in the throes of war:

'Blessed city of Athena, goddess of war-hosts, when you have seen much and endured much and toiled and suffered much, you will become an eagle among the clouds for all time.'[4]

One result of having become a pawn in Hellenic power-politics was to make the Delphians anti-Athenian at the beginning of the Peloponnesian war. They encouraged Thurii when it sought authority to throw off its spiritual allegiance to Athens as its metropolis, and when some months before the outbreak of war the Spartans consulted the oracle on the issue, the Pythian Apollo offered them his help 'when sought or unsought'.[5] It was perhaps the last occasion on which the Delphic oracle was to be consulted by a Greek state on a major political issue, unconnected with cult or ritual. The Greeks soon saw the grim fulfilment of this prophecy in the ravages of the plague in Athens. For Homer had established the connection between Apollo and the weapon of pestilence. Some contemporaries, such as Thucydides, regarded oracular responses and their alleged fulfilments as mere illustrations of the vagaries of human behaviour, particularly under stress. But no doubt the majority of Greeks still believed in the truth of prophecy, even if they might have doubts concerning human knowledge of the gods. Herodotus, for instance, had firmly maintained that the genuineness of such forecasts was not open to question.

The effects of the war and the attitude adopted by the priests of the Pythian Apollo tended to prejudice Athens' relations with Delphi. Access to the sanctuary was cut off by land, and by sea would be difficult, while the Spartans found the place of strategic importance in their operations in central Greece. The feeling that the oracle was hostile does not show itself in Sophocles, but Euripides, more prone to be influenced by contemporary events, in several of his plays exhibits a bitter attitude towards the god. His earliest tragedies contain no special criticism of Apollo or his oracles, but somewhere in the period between the outbreak of the Peloponnesian war and the Sicilian expedition he produced the *Andromache* and the *Ion*, both notable for their pointed attacks on the Delphians and their oracle. In the former play the murder of Neoptolemus at Delphi is described with every attempt to emphasise its cowardliness and treachery. In the *Ion* the Pythian Apollo remains the villain of the piece in spite of a perfunctory attempt to excuse him in the epilogue. The later plays of Euripides, such as the *Electra*, the *Iphigeneia in Tauris* and the *Orestes*, though less marked in this tendency, contain in places some sharp jibes at Apollo.

In these circumstances it is not surprising to find that the Athenians began to consult other oracle-centres. Two rivals to Delphi had begun to establish their importance in Greece. Dodona and Ammon had both been the recipients of hymns composed by Pindar. Both were regarded as oracles of Zeus himself. Dodona had a history, which as we have seen, reached back to Homer, but it had probably not been consulted previously by states as distant from it as Athens. Ammon at the oasis of Siwa in the Libyan Desert was far more inaccessible. It could only be reached direct from the Mediterranean by a journey of two hundred miles across the waterless wastes. Evidently from the beginning of the fifth century it had come into contact with Cyrene and then with mainland Greece, particularly Sparta and Athens. The cult of Ammon in the oasis which took its name from him was really a branch establishment from the temple of Amon-Ra in Egyptian Thebes. The inhabitants of the oasis were not Egyptians, but had apparently fallen under the control of the Pharaohs in some late Dynastic period, when the worship of the supreme god of Thebes had been established there just as it was in Nubia. The oracular methods employed appear to have been essentially the same as in Thebes. The image of Ammon in a shrine was carried on the shoulders of priests and its movements towards or away from a written enquiry laid on the ground would be interpreted as expressing the god's approval or disapproval. Consequently enquirers submitted their questions in writing and they had to frame their consultation in such a way that it could be answered by a 'yes' or 'no'.[6]

As we have seen, this procedure bears some resemblance to the method used at this time in Dodona. There also the enquiry was submitted in writing and was often framed so as to present a simple alternative. Also, in both places the god worshipped claimed to be supreme in the pantheon which no doubt partly explains why the Greeks originally chose to identify the African deity with Zeus and not with Apollo. At any rate the two sanctuaries of Epirus and Siwa apparently came to recognise each other, and the priestesses of Dodona when Herodotus visited them were prepared to approve a legend which told how each had been founded by doves which flew from Egyptian Thebes. It is likely enough that part of this willingness to seek a partner abroad lay in the fact that both had a dominant rival at Delphi. It is first during the Peloponnesian war that we find Athens consulting each of them. In the early years of the struggle her forces had to operate in the north-west at the mouth of the Corinthian Gulf. Some fragments of an inscription on bronze from Dodona record an Athenian dedication, and seem to be a memorial to a naval victory won at this time. Also at the same period the authority of Zeus was sought for the establishment in Athens of the Thracian goddess, Bendis. Probably the cult was introduced in connection with the effort to form friendly relations with King Sitalces of Thrace. At other times the subject of the establishment of a new cult would have been a typical subject for an enquiry at Delphi. The choice of Dodona therefore is significant.[7]

The ambitious plan to send an expedition to conquer Sicily was the occasion for special oracular enquiries. Delphi was once again accessible and was consulted, but so also were Dodona and Ammon. It is the first time when Athens herself is described as enquiring in the Libyan sanctuary. Traditions created after the event of course credited the priests of both the shrines of Zeus with suitable ambiguities. Actually it is much more likely that they simply had given the god's approval of the expedition.[8]

All three great oracle-centres figure together again in an episode after the end of the Peloponnesian war. Lysander who had been the architect of the Spartan victory became involved in a struggle for power with the kings of both royal houses who combined against him. He saw his only hope was to replace the hereditary kingship of Lacedaemon by an elective system which might give him an opportunity to oust one of the rulers and take his place. Such a basic change of the constitution would have been regarded as something which could not be carried out simply on secular authority. It would need divine sanction, and tradition declared that Lysander first attempted unsuccessfully to bribe the Pythia by means of some Delphian officials, and made a similar unsuccessful attempt to win over the oracle of Dodona by an agent, one Pherecrates of Apollonia. When these attempts had failed he finally tried Ammon, and this time he set out in person on a pilgrimage to the distant shrine—the first Greek of distinction whom we know to undertake this venture. He could justify his endeavour by the fact that he had a family tradition connecting him with Ammon, as shown also by his brother's name, Libys. Also he alleged that he had earlier had a dream in which the god had appeared and had warned him to abandon the siege of Aphytis. This had been the occasion for him to vow to make an expiatory pilgrimage to the shrine. But if he actually tried by fair or foul means to get oracular support, the priests of Ammon did not give him what he needed. In fact Ephorus, the fourth-century historian, alleged that the Libyans sent an embassy to protest against Lysander's plots, and after fruitless efforts the disgusted ambassadors departed from Sparta with the comment, 'We shall give a better judgment, when you come to settle in Libya', alluding to an old prophecy that the Spartans would one day send a colony there.[9]

The stories of Lysander's attempts to work the oracles may be exaggerated, as they were evidently spread to some extent by his enemies after his death. But it is likely that they have at least some foundation, and they show the extent to which the prestige of oracles was beginning to dwindle. It was still useful to obtain their support for special projects, but no one would be greatly surprised or shocked if they were in some instances the product of chicanery.

Another more bare-faced, but also more honest attempt to make use of an oracle occurred in the case of the Spartan king, Agesipolis. In 387 B.C., toward the end of the Corinthian war, the Argives evolved the trick of staving off a Spartan invasion by always proclaiming the festival of the Carneia when the enemy were about to cross the frontier. As good Dorians the Spartans could not lightly violate the sacred truce even when the festival was being celebrated quite abnormally by juggling with the calendar. So King Agesipolis after obtaining an auspicious omen from his preliminary sacrifices went to collect oracular authority for his unorthodox breach of the truce.[10] He began by consulting the oracle at Olympia which at this time was usually asked about the prospects of athletes. But he evidently chose this place because Elis had lately been conquered by Sparta and at this time was particularly subject to her pressure. Zeus gave his assent to the refusal of the truce, and, thus fortified, Agesipolis went to Delphi where he contented himself with asking Apollo whether he agreed with his father on the question, and the Pythia assented. Evidently the Spartan king's intention was to force the Delphic oracle to give its agreement by invoking its favourite dogma that Apollo was the spokesman of Zeus. Delphi at the time was not committed to the Spartan side, and Agesipolis may have had no confidence that the Pythia without its special challenge would give them support. But this sophistic treatment of the method of enquiry shows how artificial the whole business was becoming.

Private individuals, too, as well as politicians, may have been becoming more lax in their attitude. Socrates and Xenophon provide an interesting contrast in their attitudes. In Plato's *Apology* Socrates explains that he had started on his investigation of human wisdom because of a reply of the Delphic oracle.[11] His rather eccentric friend Chaerephon had once enquired of the Pythia whether any one was wiser than Socrates and had received the answer that none was wiser. As the facts were sworn to in court by Chaerephon's surviving brother, we need not doubt their basic truth. Probably Chaerephon, who was notoriously poor, had enquired by means of the lot, framing his question so as to seek an alternative answer. One may wonder that the Delphic authorities did not exercise some censorship on such a peculiar enquiry, but presumably they were unwilling to intervene between the worshipper and the god. Anyway, the Pythia's lot gave judgment that no one was wiser than Socrates, and this answer which surprised Socrates himself set him on the investigation which led him to conclude that he was wiser than other men because he knew that he knew nothing.

Such is Plato's account, and while it may be somewhat simplified so as to emphasise that Socrates' career was guided by Apollo's inspiration, one need not doubt its basic truth. Also it is easier to believe that the reply was produced by the chance drawing of a lot rather than to suppose that it represented any judgment by the Pythia or the Delphic priesthood on Socrates' reputation as a philosopher. The god's will had by the luck of the draw produced a surprising answer, but Socrates himself was acting perfectly in accordance with the view of a pious Greek when he supposed that there was a deeper meaning than the plain statement. Apollo notoriously expressed himself in ambiguous words. Yet it is strange to surmise what a difference might have been produced in the history of Greek philosophy, if the Delphic oracle had not, by whatever accidental means, given Socrates an impulse towards his dialectical investigation.

While Socrates illustrates a serious following-up of a rather quixotic enquiry, Xenophon shows a much less sincere treatment of the oracle.[12] In 401 B.C. he had received an invitation from Proxenus of Thebes to join him in Asia Minor with the prospect of serving under Cyrus. As a young Athenian already seriously compromised by his political record, Xenophon was evidently attracted by the opportunity of a career in Persian employment. However, he consulted the aged Socrates who had his doubts on the matter but advised Xenophon to go to Delphi and consult the god about the venture. Xenophon went and enquired of Apollo to which of the gods by offering sacrifice and prayer he would go best and most fairly on the journey which he had in mind and after a successful achievement return safe, and Apollo indicated to him by lot to which gods he should sacrifice. So he returned and told the oracle to Socrates. But he, when he had heard it, blamed Xenophon because he had not first asked whether it was better for him to go or to stay, but himself having decided that he should go had enquired how he might best go on his journey. 'But,' said he, 'since you have asked in that way, you must do what the god has commanded.'

Evidently Socrates sincerely believed that the Delphic oracle could give a more than human guidance in matters of doubt. But also he recognised that the human enquirer must play the game according to certain rules. It was not fair play to beg the question which one should really have asked by framing the enquiry in a form which would not admit of alternative answers. At the time Xenophon may have hoped that he had committed Apollo to guarantee him a successful expedition provided he performed certain ritual requirements. But Socrates' criticism may have convinced him of his mistaken attitude. At least he reports the reprimand as well as the occasion for it. Some years later when he had successfully come through the March of the Ten Thousand and other adventures he showed his gratitude by enquiring at Delphi about the disposal of his share of the spoils. Half he made into a dedication in the Athenian treasury at Delphi and with the other half he built a temple to Artemis 'where the god directed by his oracle'.[13]

Xenophon remained a pious man according to his lights, and deplored the decline in respect for the gods. In describing an international peace conference at Delphi in 368 B.C. he notes with disapproval that the delegates never communicated their problems to Apollo. In 355 B.C. in his last pamphlet writing as an aged man he made certain proposals for reforms and ended by suggesting that Dodona and Delphi should be consulted whether these proposals were for the good of the city and, if they agreed, then they should enquire whom of the gods to associate with the change.[14] (Evidently Xenophon had learnt by now at least his lesson from Socrates.) The fact that he chose to join Dodona to Delphi in his proposal and even to give it first place may be accounted for less by the decline in the reputation of the Pythian Apollo than in a series of practical obstacles to the consultation of the Pythia.

First, in the winter of 373 B.C., in conjunction with a severe earthquake off the northern coast of the Peloponnese, Delphi was involved in catastrophe.[15] A landslide laid low the temple, and devastated the upper part of the sacred enclosure. It was only through great efforts spread over numbers of years that the Delphic Amphictyony managed to raise enough money, partly by a levy on the Greek states and partly by private subscription, to restore the shrine. Presumably some kind of consultation could be organised by the use of lot even before the building was restored, but it would not be surprising if the proper ritual of seating the Pythia on the tripod had to be suspended for years. The work of restoration was well advanced, though not complete, when in 356 B.C. a new difficulty supervened. The Phocians who

were under pressure from Thebes seized the sanctuary and claimed
the sovereignty as in the fifth century. This led to the Third Sacred
War lasting till 346 B.C. and in its course the Phocian leaders were
driven to strip the place of its sacred offerings in gold and silver so as
to pay mercenary soldiers. They made a show of continuing the
restoration until 351 B.C. when work was suspended. When peace
came at last the progress with the building must have been slow. As
late as 352 B.C. a contractor was paid to provide 'a shelter beside the
retaining wall for those consulting the oracle', while at the same time
constructional work seems to have been going on in the neighbourhood of the omphalos in the innermost sanctuary. Hostilities broke
out again in 339 (the Fourth Sacred War) but were soon ended by the
battle of Chaeronea (338). It was probably at last in 330 B.C. that the
rebuilt temple was consecrated.

It is not surprising if in this period of forty-three years the activity
of Delphi had been seriously interrupted and its work had been transferred to its rivals. In 371 B.C., for instance, we have the first recorded
instance of an official consultation of Zeus at Dodona by the Spartans.[16]
It was a remarkable occasion when the peculiar happening led our
authorities to record the details. The Spartans had enquired about
victory in their war with Thebes,

and the ambassadors had placed together the vessel in which were the lots
when a monkey, which the king of the Molossi kept as a pet, overturned the
lots themselves and all the other things prepared for the drawing of lots
and scattered them this way and that. Then the priestess who was in charge
of the oracle is said to have told the Spartans that they ought not to be think-
ing about victories, but about saving themselves.

Our ultimate source for this account is the contemporary author,
Callisthenes. Evidently the ambassadors had submitted their question
in writing on one of the leaden strips such as have been found at
Dodona and it had been rolled up and inserted in a jar ready for its
ceremonial extraction by the priestess. But at the last moment the mis-
chievous ape had upset the preparations. However the priestess with
ready wit saw in this intervention a divine omen. The question submitted by the Spartans was absurdly inappropriate, and the god through
the animal agent had shown his contempt for it. Instead of victory
they must consider safety, and the fearful disaster of Leuctra which
followed immediately justified the conjecture.

This untoward happening did not discourage the Spartans from consulting Dodona again in the next few years. Also Athens made a number of enquiries there from the mid-fourth century onwards. Demosthenes in 347 quoted two responses from Dodona on ritual matters.[17] There is some doubt whether the texts given in our manuscripts are authentic or are instead fictitious examples supplied by ancient editors. But in either event they probably reproduce the correct form of a reply from Dodona, which is otherwise not provided by our sources:

'To the people of Athens the oracle of Zeus signifies: because you have missed the seasons for the sacrifice and the sacred embassy, he bids you send ambassadors on this account with speed; to Zeus Naïos three bulls and beside each bull two rams, to Dione a cow to offer in sacrifice and a bronze table to join the offering which the people of Athens had dedicated.'

The use of the verb 'signifies' probably implies that this oracle was evoked by drawing lots. There is nothing to suggest ecstatic prophecy in the phrasing. Presumably the enquiry had been about what gods and goddesses should be honoured. It is interesting to notice that Zeus had no hesitation in asking for offerings for himself with a sharp reminder about the delay. The other oracle which Demosthenes quotes is not so selfish. It enjoins a festival to Dionysus and offerings to Apollo the Averter and Zeus Ktesios.

In later speeches Demosthenes quotes Dodona on the need for the Athenians to be on their guard against their leaders. He used the prophecy against Aeschines, and twenty years later his opponent, Dinarchus, retorted the same prophecy against him when he in turn was on trial.[18]

There are several other references in this period to Athenian enquiries at Dodona and it is likely that the underlying causes for this choice of oracle-centres were political. After Philip of Macedon had seized the presidency of the Delphic Amphictyony in 346 B.C. Athens felt somewhat estranged. In the time of the Fourth Sacred War Aeschines could allege that Demosthenes had coined the phrase 'the Pythia has philippised'. Later again in 332 Athens had been excluded by the Delphians from consultations because it had not accepted a disqualification at the Olympic games. So negatively the Athenians may have found it often preferable not to consult the Pythian Apollo. But positively, too, the Athenians may have hoped to find political support in north-west Greece. At some date between 330 and 324 B.C. while Alexander was in Asia, Zeus of Dodona, as Hyperides records, bade them

decorate the image of Dione. So the Athenians had made a face for the image and all that went with it as beautifully as possible and had dispatched a sacred embassy with a sacrifice at great expense.'[19]

But though the Athenians had fulfilled the oracle's instructions in magnificent style, their pious act had a hostile reaction. Olympias, Alexander's mother, and at the time the regent of Epirus, sent an indignant letter to Athens, protesting that the land of the Molossi in which the sanctuary stood was hers and that the Athenians had no business to interfere with anything there. The fact that the queen took such a serious and inimical view of the Athenians' action suggests that perhaps it was not solely inspired by piety, but also by a wish to win influence in this direction.

Our literary sources do not give similar evidence for connections with Ammon, but actually there was an intensification of Athens' links with it, too, before the mid-fourth century as is shown by inscriptional evidence. In the mid-seventies at latest the treasury of Athens contained 'a silver bowl of Ammon' and in 363 a decree was inscribed ordering various offerings on behalf of the Athenian people beginning with six to Zeus Ammon.[20] This may show that already his shrine had been established in the Piraeus, where it certainly existed later. Also a few years afterwards a very fragmentary Attic inscription, restored by Woodward, contains a list of several different parties of sacred ambassadors 'who had brought the gold to Ammon'. They appear to have made this pilgrimage on the state's behalf at various times before 360 B.C. and presumably both brought this precious offering and also made enquiries. It may have been this recurring practice, not mentioned in our extant historians, which led to the remarkable step whereby in the later part of the fourth century the name Salaminia was discontinued for one of the two sacred triremes and was replaced by the name Ammonias, 'ship of Ammon'. The change had taken place by 330 B.C. or just after that date, but actually may have occurred earlier, though it has failed to find a place in our records. The most obvious explanation for the trireme's name would be that one of its regular duties was to carry sacred embassies to Africa on their way to approach the oracle.

NOTES

1. The serpent column: Herodotus, *9*, 81. The Aeginetan offering: id, *8*, 122
2. The bones of Theseus: Parke and Wormell, *2*, no. 113. Hero cults: Cleomedes of Astypalaea (victor, Olympia, 492 B.C.), id, no. 88; Euthymus (victor, Olympia, 484 B.C.) id, no. 117; Theagenes of Thasos (victor, Olympia, 480 and 476 B.C.), id, no. 389–391
3. Parke and Wormell, *2*, no. 131
4. Parke and Wormell, *2*, no. 121
5. Thucydides, *1*, 118, *3*, 123, 1 and 2, 54, 4
6. Parke, *Oracles of Zeus*, 194 ff.
7. Dittenberger, *Sylloge Inscriptionum Graecarum* no. 73. Ziehen, *Leges Graecorum Sacrae*, II, 1, no. 42
8. Delphi: Plu. *3*, 463B and *Nicias*, 13, 6; Dodona: Dio Chr. 17, 17 and Pausanias 8, 11, 12; Ammon: Plu. *Nicias*, 13 and 14, 7.
9. Plu. *Lysander*, 25. Diodorus Siculus, *14*, 13
10. Xenophon, *Hellenica*, *4*, 7
11. Plato, *Apology*, 20E and Xenophon, *Apology*, 14. cf. Parke, *Cl. Philology*, 56 (1961), 249
12. Xenophon, *Anabasis*, *3*, 1, 5
13. Xenophon, *Anabasis*, *5*, 3, 6
14. Xenophon, *Hellenica*, *7*, 1. 27 and *De Vectigalibus*, 5, 9
15. Parke and Wormell, 1, 213 ff. (the landslide) and 221 ff. (the Third Sacred War). 'The shelter . . . for those consulting the oracle', Dittenberger, *SIG*, 247
16. Cicero, *de Divinatione*, *1*, 34, 76 and 2, 32, 69 (Callisthenes, *F. Gr. Hist.* 124 f. 22)
17. Demosthenes, 21, 51
18. Demosthenes, 19, 29, and Dinarchus, 1, 78 and 79
19. 'The Pythia has philippised': Aeschines, 3, 130; exclusion from the Olympic games: Pausanias, *5*, 21, 5; Hyperides, *Eux.* 24
20. A. M. Woodward, *Annual of the British School of Athens*, 57 (1962), 5 ff.

THE HELLENISTIC PERIOD

(I) ALEXANDER

While Athens tended to seek divine authority in more distant sources, Delphi had fallen into the control of the Macedonians. Philip had used it as a valuable centre of political influence, and occasionally consulted the oracle, but there is no sign that he attached much importance to this activity. Alexander was connected by legend with the Pythia who was said to have conferred on him accidentally the title 'unconquerable', but it is doubtful whether he ever consulted her.[1] His most famous oracular enquiry was at Ammon, and has given rise to all sorts of accounts in antiquity and very varied interpretations in modern times.

After he had founded Alexandria at the western extremity of the Delta, he proceeded to lead an expedition to the oasis of Siwa. While they agree that he intended to consult the oracle, ancient accounts differ about the subject of his enquiry.[2] Callisthenes, the only writer on the question in Alexander's lifetime, apparently left the matter un-stated, and it is probable that this was Alexander's own intention that his enquiry and the answer should remain confidential. Later writers alleged that his purpose was to enquire about his ancestry, but this is part of the process of romanticising which was subsequently applied to the journey across the desert and the scene in the sanctuary.

From the point of view of the priests of Zeus it must have been a unique and highly important occasion. A Pharaoh was consulting the god in person. For Alexander, whether he actually had submitted to the official ceremonies of inauguration at the hands of Egyptian priest-hood, was certainly given the official titles. Hence he was received at

Siwa with all the ceremonial appropriate to one who was himself an incarnation of the gods. The chief priest in front of the temple correctly addressed him as 'son of Zeus'. Then Alexander passed into the shrine wearing his clothes as he was, while his attendants were required to change their dress. Also he alone received the answer to his enquiry within, the rest were answered outside. The method of enquiry was evidently that already mentioned: the god signified his approval or disapproval by the movements of his image carried on the shoulders of priests. After the ceremony was over Alexander departed, expressing himself well satisfied with the result of the consultation.

Later authorities treated the salutation of the chief priest as the god's oracle, and so regarded it that either Alexander had asked about his paternity or else that the god had spontaneously given this revelation of his divine origin. The whole scene was worked up into a dramatic dialogue between the king and the prophet. Alternatively it was pictured by those who gave a cynical twist to the history of Alexander as a sheer mistake on the part of the chief priest. He had attempted to address the king in Greek with the words 'dear son' and by a slip said 'son of Zeus'. The king had then seized on this *lapsus linguae* as an oracle. But this version is grossly unjust to both parties. Alexander as a Pharaoh was in Egyptian theory the son of Amon-Ra, and the priest, who evidently addressed him in Greek, would appear fully justified in translating this by 'Son of Zeus'. The theological implications would be quite different to an Egyptian and to a Greek, but this was because of the long and diverse theological traditions of the two civilisations.

Actually it would appear that Alexander's enquiry was in some way concerned with the success of his war against Persia. Wilcken believed that he asked for world dominion, but this view will only be acceptable to those who are convinced that this was already Alexander's conscious objective. However he phrased his question, no doubt Ammon promised him success in his venture; the oracle would do no less in answer to a conquering Pharaoh. Also associated with the response were probably instructions as to the deities to whom offering was to be made when the success was finally achieved. This much at least seems to be indicated by the later events. When Alexander reached the Indus and at last started on his homeward route he made certain solemn sacrifices which he indicated had been prescribed for him by Ammon, and this presumably referred to the occasion of his single visit to the shrine.

However, as we have seen, the more or less routine activity of enquiring for the success of a venture and receiving directions about the appropriate ritual was completely overshadowed in literary tradition and the popular imagination by the public greeting of Alexander as the son of Zeus. Whether it had any great influence on the mind of Alexander himself is not easy to prove. When some eight years later he called on the Greek states to recognise his divinity there is no sign that he based it officially on the address delivered by the chief priest. Yet it is likely that the idea would have seemed even more strange to contemporaries if the way had not been opened by the episode at Ammon. Though Alexander himself, reasonably enough, treated the cult of Zeus Ammon with respect and consulted the oracle again on such questions as the honours due to his dead friend, Hephaestion, there is no sign that the shrine became any more frequented by Greeks than previously: if anything, less. One consultation in the reign of Ptolemy Soter is recorded and he honoured the god with a dedication, and after that it drops out of our tradition as a practical source of enquiry.[3]

(2) THE RISE OF THE LOCAL ORACLE-CENTRES

In other directions, however, Alexander's conquests produced a permanent effect. His campaigns had completely shifted the centre of gravity of the Greek world. Instead of being based in Hellas, it was now spread over much of nearer Asia and into Egypt. The first to benefit from this change were the traditional centres of Greek oracles in Asia Minor. We have seen how at the end of the Ionian revolt, when Miletus fell, the temple of Apollo Didymeus at Branchidae had been sacked, and its consultations had been suppressed. After Alexander freed Asia Minor from Persian dominion, the sanctuary was revived. As Strabo comments, Callisthenes, Alexander's contemporary chronicler,

adds to his dramatic writing-up of the visit to Ammon the statement that 'Apollo had abandoned the oracle at Branchidae when the sanctuary had been plundered by the Branchidae who had joined the Persian side under Xerxes, and the spring even had failed, but at that time the spring shot up and many prophecies were brought by the Milesian embassies to Memphis concerning the birth of Alexander from Zeus and the victory that was to occur at Arbela and the death of Dareius and the revolutionary movements in Sparta.'[4]

No doubt this sensational account was produced by Callisthenes after the defeat and assassination of the Persian king and the oracular utterances had been suitably interpreted after these events. However in spite of some rhetorical exaggeration there is a basis of fact, in that the ancient Apolline sanctuary began to be restored and evidently at an early stage made a grand demonstration of loyalty towards Alexander who had given it a new lease of life. The plans for the new temple were laid out on a truly colossal scale, larger than any existing Greek religious building. Its immediate predecessor in archaic times had been a large structure, but was completely outclassed. A consequence of the grandiose planning was that the work was never finished. Building continued at intervals through the Hellenistic and even the Roman imperial period and while much was carried out the full scale of the work was never accomplished.

Branchidae was not the only Ionian oracle to claim associations with Alexander. At Claros, near Colophon, was a very old site of an Apolline sanctuary. It had legendary traditions of the prophets of the Trojan war, so we can no doubt suppose that its activities had included an oracle, though this fact is not preserved in our literary sources. However, with the re-establishment of Greek freedom it sprang into greater prominence and became one of the chief oracular centres of later times. It claimed the credit for the re-establishment of Smyrna on its new Hellenistic site. As the legend went, Alexander while hunting on Mount Pagus slept under a plane-tree and in a dream the two goddesses of fate (the Nemeseis) appeared to him and told him to remove the Smyrneans and settle them there.[5] So the people of Smyrna sent an embassy to Claros to ask about the situation and the god gave them an oracle in verse:

> Thrice blest will they be, yea four times blest who
> shall dwell on Pagus beyond the holy river, Meles.

So the inhabitants removed across the river to its new site. One notes that the priests of Claros were like Delphi in issuing their replies in hexameter verse and not merely giving a 'yes' or 'no' answer to an alternative question.

The desire of the newly revived oracles of Ionia to link themselves to the new Hellenistic monarchies is illustrated in the two other hexameter responses in which Branchidae claimed to have prophesied the kingship of Seleucus Nicator and his death in Macedon.[6] The latter contained the usual equivocation whereby the recipient of the prophetic warning did not recognise its true application till too late.

Thus we find the oracle-centres of Apollo in Asia stepping into the old traditional functions of the Delphic oracle. They provided authority for the settlement of a city or foretold the accession and the death of a ruler. These somewhat legendary examples are symptomatic of the process that was to take place in the Hellenistic period. The oracle-centres in the new Greek lands were revived or created, sometimes by identifying a native deity and cult with an Hellenic god. These nearer shrines in their own territory claimed successfully the custom of the new communities. Delphi was far off and also unfortunately fell into a very definite political association. From the beginning of the third century B.C. the Pythian sanctuary was taken over by the Aetolian league, one of those new federations which were a feature of the period. Its membership spread to include such distant states as Chios, but the very success of its political expansion probably tended to discourage those from outside from using the Pythian Apollo. Anyway it would generally be true to state that at this time kings and communities rarely consulted oracles on major questions of state. Their usual enquiries would concern matters of cult. But also at times this category of question could be extended to new fields. For instance the practice developed of asking the Pythia to give a response recognising a territory as 'free from plunder' (Asylon).[7] This had the effect of declaring it to be a demilitarised zone and in theory was based on the sanctity of the locality because of its associations with some deity. In practice it was a convenient way in which a small city might be declared neutral in the recurrent struggles of the professional armies of the Hellenistic kings. Delphi was the special source of these pronouncements and the reason may have been that even under Aetolian suzerainty it still had a wider international reputation than other oracle-centres.

Though enquiries from kings and city-states may have been less frequent in the Hellenistic period there is no sign that the total amount of private enquiries was any less than in the classical period. Dodona, for instance, where the lead tablets preserve the private individual's questions shows a considerable proportion of probably third-century date. It is often suggested that the cults of the state deities were losing their hold on the popular faith, and this may be true. But oracles seem still to have fulfilled a need. Also the rise of the new philosophies did not necessarily harm the belief in prophecy. The Academics as followers of Socrates could not well discount oracles entirely and Aristotle had had close associations with Delphi. Still more the Stoics with their strong belief in fate were prepared to accept the possibility that the future could be foreseen. It was only the Epicureans, with their view of a world governed by chance and gods who had no care for humanity, who were committed to a philosophy completely opposed to oracles.

So though our evidence from literary sources is very patchy it is probably right to suppose that the business of consulting the gods at their shrines was still busily followed. The classic centre of Delphi may have had less to do, but it was partly because there was a proliferation of local shrines which catered for their own neighbourhoods. For instance on the acropolis of Argos was an old sanctuary of Apollo Pythaeus. It had dated from the archaic period and may have been an oracle-centre in early times, but actually our only evidence (literary and epigraphic) is from the third century B.C. when it seems to have worked up some local connection in the Peloponnese.[8] Delphi was dominated by the Aetolian league with which Argos and her neighbouring states had no association. Typically enough the traditional legend explained the cult-title by alleging that its founder was Pythaeus, a son of Apollo, who had come to Argos from Delphi. But the ritual practice was different. There is no talk of a spring or a tripod, nor of a chasm. Once a month the prophetess—for as at Delphi she was a woman who must abstain from sexual intercourse—tasted the blood of lamb sacrificed by night, and so was inspired to speak under the possession of Apollo.

Another example of the revival of a local oracle is known from an inscription found at Corope in Thessaly on the lower slopes of Mount Pelion.[9] There had evidently been a temple of Apollo there from early periods. It has scarcely left its mark in literature, but at the beginning of the first century B.C., when it had fallen under the control of the Hellenistic city of Demetrias, an elaborate effort was made to revive the operation of the oracle in a more regular and dignified manner. It is implicit that the consultations had previously been held in a disorderly way and the inscribed regulations are to tighten up the ceremonial. In a preamble the devotion of the city to Apollo Coropaeus is recorded because he, 'reveals through the oracle in common and privately to individuals on the subject of what concerns health and safety' [and it is explained that since] 'the oracle is ancient and held in special regard by our ancestors and since more strangers are coming to visit the prophetic sanctuary, it has been decided that the city should take more careful foresight of the good organisation of the oracle'. [The regulations stipulate that the procession is to consist of] 'the priest of Apollo named by the city and one each of the officers of the generals and the guardians of the laws, and one member of the council (*prytanis*) and a treasurer and the secretary of the god and the prophet. If any of the afore-mentioned is sick or absent abroad, let him send another [in his place]. The generals and the guardians of the laws are to enrol three "rod-holders" from the citizens, men younger than thirty years of age, who are to have authority to restrain the disorderly'. [Provision was made for a daily wage for these beadles and for them to be fined heavily for non-attendance.] 'Whenever the afore-mentioned have arrived at the oracle-centre and have completed the sacrifice in the ancestral fashion and have obtained good omens, the clerk of the god after the sacrifice is to receive the written entries of those who wish to consult the oracle and is to record the names on a black-board and exhibit the black-board at once in front of the temple and bring them in calling them up in the order of the record, unless any have permission to enter first, and if he who is called up is not present let him bring in the next, until he who is called up arrive. The afore-mentioned are to be seated in the sanctuary in bright robes garlanded with the wreaths of laurel, ritually pure and sober, and they are to receive the tablets from the enquirers at the oracle. Whenever the oracle has been accomplished, they are to put the tablets into the receptacle and seal it down with the seal of the generals and the guardians of the laws, and also the seal of the priest, and they are to let it remain in the sanctuary. At dawn the secretary of the god is to produce the receptacle and show the seals to the afore-mentioned and then to open it and give back the tablets to each calling them up from the record.'

Unfortunately at this point the inscription is broken and nothing more is preserved of this decree except some more regulations about the 'rod-holders'.

The modern reader would have been interested to know more about the oracular procedure itself and less about the discipline. Particularly it is left quite obscure at what point in the proceedings and how the enquirers got the answers to their written enquiries. Stählin was prepared to believe that by some fraudulent method answers were written on to the tablets during the night and were then produced from an apparently sealed container the next morning. But most scholars would agree with Robert that there is no indication to support this on the decree and it is most unlikely that the magistrates of a Hellenistic city lent themselves to such a naive imposture.[10] The problem of exact procedure used in the consultation remains insoluble. For our present purpose the inscription is significant as an illustration of the systematic revival of a local oracle in conjunction with the civic organisation of a neighbouring city. Though the preamble refers to the consultation of Apollo by communities as well as private individuals in the past, the new rules contain no provisions for enquirers representing cities. Probably such consultations were not to be expected. But if the preamble is to be trusted as evidence 'more strangers' were coming. Perhaps this was as much a development of tourist traffic as of religious enquirers. But evidently it had become the occasion for a tightening-up of the regulations and a new control of disorderly behaviour.

Other instances of the development of local prophetic cults offer more peculiar examples of strange practices. At Ephyre on the coast of Epirus there was a shrine dedicated to enquiries from the dead. Herodotus records a grimly picturesque story of an embassy sent to consult it by Periander, the tyrant of Corinth, when he was answered by the wife whom he had murdered. The out-of-the-way shrine scarcely occurs elsewhere in our literary tradition, but S. I. Dakaris has lately found what is evidently the place.[11] His excavations disclose a building which was clearly enlarged in the Hellenistic period and seems to have been surprisingly large and thriving for such an isolated spot. The completion of the excavation and its publication will no doubt fill in much detail. But one intriguing find consists in a number of massive bronze rackets and pinions which suggest that in the later periods at least by some mechanical contrivance some kind of a *deus ex machina* may have been produced to frighten and impress enquirers.

Another local shrine which must have had primitive origins but appears to have risen in importance in the third century was that of Trophonius at Lebadeia in Boeotia. He was a chthonic deity, originally active in the sphere of fertility as his name suggests. But by the fifth century B.C. at latest he was already being consulted by a unique method of which we have a detailed account in Pausanias the traveller.[12] It is our only fully circumstantial narrative of the procedure of an oracle recorded by an actual enquirer. For Pausanias, evidently well aware of the remarkable character of the subject, states that he himself had consulted Trophonius and had seen others who had done so. Of course, his enquiry will have been made about the middle of the second century A.D. and the procedure which he describes shows features of sophistication which are not likely to go back to primitive times. But it is probable that the main lines of the practice had been laid down in the Hellenistic period and the central idea of going underground to consult Trophonius occurs in our earliest references.

As Pausanias describes it:

when a man has resolved to go down to the oracle of Trophonius, he first of all lodges for a stated number of days in a certain building which is sacred to the Good Daemon and Good Fortune. During his sojourn there he observes rules of purity, and, in particular, refrains from warm baths. His bath is the river Hercyna; and he gets plenty of flesh from the sacrifices; for he who goes down sacrifices both to Trophonius himself and to the children of Trophonius, also to Apollo, Cronus, Zeus surnamed the King, Hera the charioteer, and Demeter whom they surname Europe and say she was Trophonius' nurse. At every sacrifice a soothsayer is present who inspects the entrails of the victim, and, having done so, foretells the person descending whether Trophonius will receive him kindly and graciously. Now the entrails of all the other victims put together do not reveal the disposition of Trophonius so well as do those of a ram which, on the night when the man goes down, they sacrifice over a pit, calling upon Agamedes. Though all the former sacrifices may have been favourable, it is no matter unless the entrails of this ram tell the same tale: if they do, then the man goes down with good hope.

The way in which he goes down is this. First of all, in the course of the night, two sons of citizens, about thirteen-years-old, lead him to the river Hercyna, and there anoint him with oil and wash him. These boys are called Hermae . . . next he is led by the priests, not at once to the oracle, but to certain springs of water, which are very near each other. Here he must drink what is called the water of Forgetfulness [Lethe], in order that he may forget everything that he has hitherto thought of. After that he drinks another water, that of Memory, whereby he remembers what he sees down below. Then after having beheld the image which they say Daedalus made (it is not shown by the priests except to such as are about to visit Trophonius), having seen and worshipped it and prayed, he comes to the oracle clad in a linen tunic girt with ribbons and shod with boots of the country. The oracle is above the grove on the mountain. It is surrounded in a circle by a basement of white marble, the circumference of which is about that of a threshing floor of the smallest size, and the height less than three feet. On the floor are set bronze spikes connected by cross-rails, which are also of bronze, and there are gates in the railing. Inside the enclosure is a chasm in the earth, not a natural chasm, but built in the exactest style of masonry. The shape of the structure is like that of a pot for baking bread in. Its breadth across may be guessed at six feet, while its depth cannot be estimated at more than twelve. There is no passage leading down to the bottom; but when a man goes to Trophonius they bring him a narrow and light ladder. When he has descended he sees a hole between the masonry and the ground: the breadth of the hole appears to be eighteen inches and its depth nine. So he lays himself on his back on the ground, and holding in his hand barley cakes kneaded with honey, he thrusts his feet first into the hole and follows himself, endeavouring to get his knees through the hole. When they are through, the rest of his body is immediately dragged after them, and shoots in, just as a man might be dragged down by a swirl of a mighty and rapid river. Once they are inside the shrine the future is not revealed to all in one and the same way, but to one it is given to see, and to another to hear. They return through the same aperture feet foremost. . . . When a man has come up from Trophonius the priests take him in hand again and set him on what is called the chair of memory, which stands not far from the shrine; and, being seated there, he is questioned by them as to all he saw and heard. On being informed, they hand him over to his friends, who carry him, still overpowered with fear, and quite unconscious of himself and his surroundings, to the building where he lodged before, the house of Good Fortune and the Good Daemon. Afterwards, however, he will have all his wits as before, and the power of laughter will come back to him.

This extraordinary narrative is certainly to be taken literally. Pausanias was obviously a sincere and honest writer with a special interest in oracles. The formidable experience had evidently impressed him greatly. Tantalisingly enough he gives no information on the subject of his own enquiry or his actual experience within the shrine of Trophonius itself. He says that all who have gone down to Trophonius are obliged to set up a tablet containing a record of what they heard or saw, but these documents, presumably on wood, have not survived. The elaborate preliminary ritual must have served both to get a suitable enquirer into a properly submissive mood and have given the priests an opportunity to reject any unsuitable subjects. Pausanias records what was evidently one of their cautionary tales, meant to encourage the timid and frighten the over-bold. They said that,

none of those who went down died, except one of Demetrius' bodyguard, who observed none of the rules of the sanctuary and went down not to consult the god, but in the hope of carrying off gold and silver from the shrine.

His dead body emerged at another opening.

In essence the method of consultation is the highly primitive custom which we have already described of entering a cavern so as to consult a power of the earth itself. Only here the operation has been worked up into a veritable ordeal. Some features, also, suggest a late and sophisticated cult—the way in which Trophonius has been fitted into a sacrificial plan associating him with the Olympian gods, the later titles such as Good Daemon and Good Fortune, and the springs of Forget-fulness and Memory which suggest some of the mystery cults. But these are only superficial additions, the result of a gradual building-up of the primitive ritual on Hellenistic lines. The core of the procedure was very ancient.

One may wonder at the fact that people could be found to undergo the trying experience. But actually it would appear that it was reason-ably frequented in the Hellenistic and Roman periods. Perhaps the very fact that the ritual turned so much on the performance of the individual enquirer fitted the Hellenistic age which, in contrast to previous times, was less an epoch of social activities than one where the individual counted as such.

NOTES

1. Parke and Wormell, *Delphic Oracle*, *1*, 240
2. For a detailed discussion and references, Parke, *Oracles of Zeus*, pp. 222 ff.
3. Alexander's enquiry about Hephaestion: Arrian, *7*, 14, 7 and 23, 6. The Rhodians' enquiry about Ptolemy: Diodorus Siculus, *20*, 100, 3; Ptolemy's dedication: Pausanias, *9*, 16, 1
4. Strabo, *17*, 1, 43 (Callisthenes, *F. Gr. Hist.* 124 f. 14)
5. Pausanias, *7*, 5, 1
6. Appian, *Syrian Wars*, 9, 56, and 10, 63
7. Parke and Wormell, 1, 371
8. Pausanias, 2, 42, 1 and e.g. Schwyzer 29. For the site W. Vollgraff, *Le sanctuaire d'Apollon Pythéen à Argos* (1950)
9. Dittenberger, *Sylloge Inscriptionum Graecarum*, 1157
10. Stählin, Pauly-Wissowa, Korope: L. Robert, *Hellenica*, 5 (1948), 16 ff.
11. Herodotus, *5*, 92. *Das Totenorakel bei Ephyra*, S. I. Dakaris, *Antike Kunst*, 1963, 51 ff.
12. For early references, e.g. Aristophanes, *Clouds*, 506, Paus. 9, 39, 5 ff.

E

1 2

THE ORACLES UNDER THE ROMANS

(1) ROME AND DELPHI

Towards the end of the third century B.C. a new factor came into Greek divination. The Romans formed contact with mainland Greece. It was the first time that this had occurred on any large scale. Legend later told how, three centuries before, the Tarquins had enquired at Delphi, and it would not have been impossible for Etruscan cities to have consulted Apollo, as the presence of a treasury dedicated by Caere shows.[1] But there is nothing dependable in the Roman legend. More genuine is the fact that after the fall of Veii at the beginning of the fourth century B.C. the Romans in gratitude had sent a gold mixing bowl to be dedicated in the sanctuary. The bowl itself was melted down in the Third Sacred War, but the bronze base on which it had stood survived long after in the treasury of the Massaliotes. The legendary oracles associated with the dedication are fictitious, and we cannot now tell what exactly was the cause for the Romans to send the offering to Apollo. Delphi might have been consulted on the issue of the war with Veii and have given a favourable answer which was acknowledged in this way after victory had been won. But, if so, no correct version of the oracular response has survived.

Rome does not appear to have maintained any regular contact with Delphi in the interval. A few dubious traditions point to the possibility that there may have been an occasional consultation, but even this is doubtful. However, with 216 B.C. we reach solid ground. After the succession of disasters in the Second Punic War leading up to the battle of Cannae, Quintus Fabius Pictor was sent to Delphi to enquire about the proper ritual to secure victory over the Carthaginians. The account of his mission is ultimately derived from his own account, for he became the first Roman historian.[2] The Pythia supplied him with a list of gods and goddesses to whom a solemn festival of supplication was to be directed in a manner prescribed and also delivered to him an oracle in Greek verse of which a Latin prose translation is preserved. This vaguely promised victory in due course if the ritual was carried out and also enjoined on the Romans the need to send gifts to Apollo from their booty. (This kind of begging oracle is first evidenced for Delphi in the mid-fourth century.)

The purpose of the Romans in consulting Delphi was probably twofold. In the depressed state of public morale after the succession of defeats it was necessary to satisfy the people that proper ritual remedies were being applied. Hence an elaborate piece of public ceremonial carried out in accordance with the directions of a distant oracle was just what was needed. The proceedings were carried through in this spirit. For instance on his return from Delphi Fabius himself read translations of the oracular responses to the people—an unusual procedure. But also the Senate may have hoped to build up better associations with the Aetolians as the masters of Delphi, and we find that soon after they emerge as Rome's allies against Philip V of Macedon and Hannibal. Connections with Delphi continued to the end of the Second Punic War. In 207 B.C. after the victory of the Metaurus ambassadors were sent to Delphi with a gold crown and some silver figures as a gift from the spoils of Hasdrubal. The Pythia responded with prophecies of greater victories. Soon afterwards Delphi was consulted over an alleged instruction in the Sibylline books to fetch the Mother of the Gods (*Magna Mater*) to Rome, and the oracle supported the plan and recommended that it could be achieved through King Attalus of Pergamum, who had close association with the Pythian sanctuary. Once more we see Delphi used both as the authority for the introduction of a new and exciting cult and as the agent for friendly contact with a possible ally.[3]

Thus in the time of her first endeavours to obtain a foothold in Greece the Roman government had found the Delphic oracle useful. But with the ending of the Second Punic War the need to adopt this method ceased. The Romans did not require any more spiritual support from Delphic prescriptions for ritual, and they were able to enforce their will on Greek states without the medium of an oracle. Delphi is not consulted again by official embassies. Individual Romans such as Sulla or Cicero could enquire of the Pythia if they happened to visit Greece, but the Roman state did not make use of Apollo again. The fact that they soon fell out with the Aetolian League may be partly responsible. But evidently to the Roman government later Delphi was mainly useful as a place which owing to its central position in Greece was particularly convenient for issuing proclamations or publishing legislation. But this activity had no direct connection with the oracle. Also the growing dominance of Rome made any enquiries by other governments superfluous. King Perseus of Macedon is the last Hellenistic king who is recorded as enquiring of the Pythia.[4] Similarly the brutal and thorough sacking of Epirus by the Romans in 189 B.C. seems to have led to the virtual extinction of the oracle of Zeus of Dodona.

The fact was that the Romans themselves had their own methods of divination and did not need Greek oracles, except in very special circumstances. For the general purpose of ascertaining whether the gods were favourable or not the Romans had their native system of augury. The members of the college of augurs could either take note of chance omens, particularly from the flight and cries of birds, or if they wished to obtain a precise answer they could designate a field of observation (*templum*) and determine divine approval or disapproval by the indications given in it. If the state was not satisfied with these methods (which were an elaboration and standardisation of the simple practices found in Homer) the senate had a tradition of calling in *Haruspices* from Etruria. The Etruscans had developed to a high degree a pseudo-science of observations of the entrails of victims read in conjunction with the movements of the heavenly bodies. This foreign procedure would be invoked in emergencies when it would give a more elaborate response than could be obtained from augury. Finally the Roman state had the Sibylline books. This collection of prophecies was written in Greek hexameters and was traditionally believed, as we have seen, to have been bought by Tarquinius Superbus from the Cumaean Sibyl. The books were regarded as containing a dangerously significant forecast of fate. So they were entrusted to the custody of the *Decemviri Sacris Faciundis* and might only be approached after a motion of the senate had given sanction. The particular instances recorded in late Republican history usually suggest that the Sibylline oracles lent themselves particularly well to manipulation for political ends. It was in fact as though the senate had a Greek oracle permanently under its control, and it is not surprising in these circumstances that the Roman government did not unnecessarily send embassies to consult other sources of prophecy. That this had an effect on the functioning of oracle-centres is actually stated by Strabo. He is discussing the neglect of Ammon in his day and remarks:

Among the ancients both divination in general and oracles were held in greater honour, but now great neglect of them prevails, since the Romans are satisfied with the oracles of the Sibyls and with the Tyrrhenian prophecies obtained by means of the entrails of animals, the flight of birds and omens from the sky.[5]

There were a few oracle-centres in Italy, outside Rome itself and of native origin. The most famous were the temples of the goddess Fortune at Praeneste and at Antium. Their method appears to have been the drawing of lots. Those of Praeneste were written on oak tablets and kept in a chest of olive-wood, both of which had pious legends to explain their origins. The Italian *sortes* seem usually not to have been mere indications of 'yes' or 'no', but to have had whole sentences written on them in which a meaning appropriate to the enquiry must be found. For instance Livy records as an omen in 218 B.C. that one lot fell of its own accord from a bundle and proved to contain the sentence: 'Mars brandishes his spear'. The appropriateness in time of this was obvious. A number of oblong bronze tablets from north Italy are actually preserved containing single sentences of a moralising or epigrammatic character and in a style suggesting archaic verse. They are probably a collection of such *sortes*. Though, as Livy shows, prodigies involving lots would be reported to the Senate as ominous, the Roman state did not use these methods or consult the Fortunes of Praeneste or Antium. They were evidently kept going, in later times at least, by private inquirers.[6]

(2) THE DECLINE OF GREEK ORACLES

In general terms one would describe the period of the late Roman Republic as the age of secularism. It was a time when in Rome even the religious ritual of the state was allowed to fall into neglect, and social custom appears to have ceased to press individuals to conform. There is no indication that the climate of opinion in the other great centres of population in the Mediterranean world was at all different. The one movement which was apparently expanding at the time was the practice and belief of astrology. This pseudo-science had started in the Orient on the basis of Babylonian observations of the heavenly bodies. Coming west in the Hellenistic period it was wedded to Greek mathematics and was in a unique position to appeal to the intelligentsia as a rational explanation of the working of fate. Nigidius Figulus (who was praetor in 58 B.C.) is the first Roman to be distinguished as a writer on astrology, and from his time 'the Chaldaeans' or 'mathematicians' who cast horoscopes were a prominent element in Roman society. Juvenal while treating Delphi as reduced to silence compared the prestige in which the astrologer was held by Roman wives to that of the oracle of Ammon.[7] Though Juvenal was exaggerating when he pictured the Pythia as silenced, it is probable that its activity reached its lowest ebb in the late Republican and early imperial periods. The Julio-Claudian emperors generally paid little attention to Delphi. Nero visited it in his notorious tour of the Greek festivals and traditionally received an ambiguous oracle which warned him against his successor, Galba. But this was no doubt fabricated *post eventum*. Apollo had no occasion to be grateful to Nero, for already before his visit he had caused some five hundred bronze statues to be removed from the sanctuary to decorate his new palace, the Golden House. The emperor is said to have been so pleased with the Pythia's answer that he bestowed a gift of 100,000 sesterces on the sanctuary which was afterwards recovered by Galba for the Roman treasury. The Flavians showed a little more patronage, but the reduced prestige of the oracle is well illustrated by two of Plutarch's dialogues.[8]

In the earlier of these—*On the decline of oracles*—the philosophic author introduces a discussion why this method of prophecy has died out in all but one or two instances.

Why need one give other examples, when Boeotia as far as oracle-centres are concerned was once so rich in voices in previous times, but now the springs, as it were, have quite failed and great dearth of prophecy has spread over the land? For nowhere else now than at Lebadeia does Boeotia provide to those who need it a draught of prophecy.

The speaker names as Boeotian centres now extinct the shrine of

Amphiaraus, that of Apollo Ptoios and that of Apollo at Tegyra. Elsewhere another speaker contrasts the situation at Delphi in the present
with its glorious past.

When at the will of the god, Greece was rich in cities and the country had
abundant inhabitants, they used to employ two prophetesses in the sanctuary in turn with a third assigned to be in reserve. Now, however, there is one
prophetess, and we have no fault to find, for she suffices the enquirers. So
one must not blame the god. For what prophecy is present and surviving is
enough for all, and all are sent away after they have received the responses
which they sought.[9]

Thus Plutarch encouraged a placid acceptance of the decline and dis-
appearance of oracles as suited to the shift of population in the Graeco-
Roman world. As an effective cause he was inclined to seek an explanation in the theory that oracular inspiration came as vapour from
the earth. In the passage of time the vapour might become used up or
change its direction. Alternatively if the inspiration was thought of as
coming from a supernatural being, it would not, of course, have been
acceptable to Greek thought that Apollo, the immortal, should grow
old and die. But one of the developments of the Hellenistic period had
been an increased belief in the agency of minor supernatural powers.
These *daemones* were pictured as possessed of potencies much beyond
the human and also as far surpassing them in length of life. But even
they might die: and the failure of an oracular-centre could be explained
by the suppositions that the *daemon* who had operated it as the agent
of Apollo had at last succumbed.

In his later treatise (the *de Pythiae oraculis*) written probably in old
age and when he had already been the priest of Apollo at Delphi for
many years Plutarch attempted to give the inspiration a more spiritual
quality. To Greek thought there was always a great difficulty in con-
ceiving the existence of anything completely immaterial. Even the soul
was pictured as made of some extremely fine substance. So Plutarch's
evidence for the existence of the vapour is confined to a description of
the sweet scent flowing from the *adyton*, which we have already
mentioned.[10] But he does not indicate the existence of any cleft
in the ground or other precise source of this manifestation, nor
as we saw does he explain how, if it was the cause of inspiration, it
did not affect the enquirers as well as the Pythia if they were aware
of it.

The treatise itself is somewhat more optimistic in its treatment of the oracle. Its subject itself is 'why the Pythia does not now prophecy in verse'. So though it dealt with a decline in the literary quality of the responses, it did not suggest that the oracle itself was ceasing. Actually the use of verse as a form had been decreasing since the early Hellenistic period. Plutarch sees the change as appropriate to the different level of importance maintained by the enquiries.

The existing affairs of the present about which they ask the god are such as I myself am content with and even welcome. There is deep peace and quiet; war has ceased, and migrations and civil strife exist no more, nor tyrannies, nor the other diseases and plagues of Greece which needed as it were the resources of many and powerful medicines. But when there is nothing complicated, nor confidential, nor terrible, but the enquiries are on trivial and vulgar affairs like the problems in school exercises 'Is one to marry?' 'Is one to go a voyage?' 'Is one to give a loan?' and the greatest prophecies given to cities are concerning crops and the fertility of cattle and bodily health, then to surround it with metre and mould it in metaphors and introduce strange expressions into enquiries needing a simple and concise reply is the work of an ambitious sophist tricking out an oracular response for the sake of his reputation.[11]

So the aged priest of Apollo was prepared to produce a defence of the plain prose answer to the contemporary enquirer.

He also found cause for hopefulness and confidence in recent developments at Delphi.

Just as with thriving trees a sapling grows beside them, so also the suburb of Pylaea flourishes with Delphi and springs up together with it on account of the prosperity derived from it receiving a plan and shape and being fitted out with temples and meeting halls and fountains, in a way such as it did not receive in the previous millennium. . . . To us Apollo produces more shining and greater and clearer signs than these, as though after drought he had replaced our former desolation and poverty by prosperity and brilliance and honour.

This marvellous change was probably due in great part to the patronage of the emperor Hadrian, who did much for Delphi together with the rest of mainland Greece. He even consulted the oracle and received a reply in hexameter verse. But it is typical enough that he did not enquire about any question of imperial policy. His gesture of respect to Apollo consisted in asking the literary conundrum: where was Homer from and what were his parents? The Pythia gave an unexpected answer, that he was born in Ithaca and his father and mother were Telemachus, the son of Odysseus, and Epicaste, the daughter of Nestor.[12]

If the Delphic oracle as well as the town had a certain degree of renaissance under Hadrian it appears to have been of limited degree and belief. But elsewhere in the Greek world Apolline oracles were highly prosperous and active.

(3) THE ORACLES OF ASIA MINOR

There was no area in the Roman empire which prospered more than Asia Minor as a result of the Augustan peace. The old Greek colonies and even more the new foundations of the Hellenistic kings throve in wealth and population. As centres of trade and manufacture they ranked among the most important in the empire. While mainland Greece had largely sunk into a backwater, the Asiatic Greeks were in the full current of contemporary life. This increase in population and prosperity was mirrored in the growth in importance of the oracle-centres of Asia, particularly the Apolline sanctuaries of Claros and Didyma. In the sixth century B.C. the Greek colonies had chiefly looked to Delphi, in the second century A.D. they looked to their own shrines.

Of these developments that of Claros is the most striking. It figures little in literature. Its first appearance in the Imperial period was in A.D. 18 when it was visited by Germanicus on his journey to the east. Tacitus, who reports the incident, appears to regard the oracle as a quaint episode in the Imperial progress and not a place generally known to Romans. He explains that the oracles are given by a man, not as at Delphi by a woman, and that the prophet is chosen from some specified families and regularly fetched from Miletus. His procedure was to ascertain the name and number of the enquirers only, but not apparently the subject of their consultation. Then he retired into a cave and after drinking a draught from a hidden spring he produced replies in formal verses on the subjects which each enquirer had in mind. Tacitus emphasises the remarkable nature of the performance by stating that the priest who uttered these oracles was mostly untaught in literature and poetry; so it was implied that his words were produced by direct inspiration. The description ends by saying that it was told that to Germanicus his approaching death was foretold in riddles as is the wont of oracles.[13]

It is not clear whether Tacitus in giving this account is reproducing some earlier source describing Germanicus' consultation, or had actually visited the place himself. As a proconsul of Asia, and a man very aware of his position as a Quindecemuir Sacris Faciundis Tacitus might be expected to have gone to the sanctuary. If so, the account which he gives (dating at latest from about A.D. 115) seems to show a condition before the great flowering of the oracle in the second century. Our later evidence does not suggest the dependence on Miletus implied in the statement that the prophet might be sought from there. Also the spontaneous production of verse by an unlettered prophet is at variance with the later records of an official actually described as a poet.

Our best evidence for the functioning of the oracle comes from the inscriptional records at the site itself.[14] Some of these have long been known, but they have been greatly increased in number and significance by the excavations of Louis Robert, starting in 1950. Unfortunately his official publication is not yet available, and until it appears scholars must depend on summary accounts of the finds. He has discovered and brought to light the temple, a building in Doric style of the third century B.C. and later. Like the temple at Didyma it was conceived on a colossal scale and probably never fully completed. The peristyle was finished in the reign of the emperor Hadrian who judging from an inscription on the architrave had contributed to this culmination.

Much more significant, however, than the general plan of the temple is the remarkable arrangement in its basement. Two staircases descended from the *pronaos* and after running parallel for some distance converged to form a single vaulted corridor leading to what was evidently the innermost sanctuary. As Robert has suggested, this must be the 'cave' mentioned by Tacitus into which the prophet retired to seek inspiration. The inscriptions from Claros similarly indicate that the rites included ceremonies appropriate to such subterranean settings. They record that sacred ambassadors 'after having been initiated entered in'—no doubt to the hidden recesses of the temple.

These inscriptional records, of which Robert has found vast additional numbers, were a special feature of the temple of Claros. As a form of homage to Apollo cities which sent sacred embassies to consult the oracle recorded their visits by inscribing on the temple a minute of the occasion. The votive notices date from the second century A.D. and the early part of the third, and show that the oracle was visited by embassies from cities to an extent which could not be imagined on the evidence of our literary texts. The building was thickly covered with inscribed records, not merely on its walls but also on the steps and even on the columns. This refutes any notion that oracles in general were in disrepute in the later imperial period. The comparative obscurity of Delphi was evidently not typical of the Asia Minor sanctuaries.

Typical entries begin with the name of the city, and date the occasion by the list of the participating officials. These consist of the *Prytanis* or presiding magistrate of Colophon, the prophet, the priest, the *Thespiodos* or singer of the oracle and the secretaries. The entry often indicated that the embassy was concerned in more than the mere process of consulting the god. References to mysteries occur and also the embassy was often accompanied by a choir of young men or even of young women who sung a special hymn to Apollo. Since the name of the hymn's composer is sometimes recorded these seem to have been special anthems produced for the occasion.

The picture to be derived from the inscriptions is of a much more elaborate and sophisticated ceremonial than that suggested by Tacitus. As we have noted there is no indication of officials fetched from Miletus, and the unlettered prophet speaking spontaneous verse is replaced by two officials, a prophet who presumably produced the actual response and a *thespiodos* who would reproduce it in metre and sing it. Here it is worth remarking that for this period at least there is evidence that the oracle went in for a certain elaboration of metrical form. Delphi throughout its history confined itself almost entirely to dactylic hexameters and the oracles of Didyma after its restoration are in that form. But Claros appears to have passed through a development. The earliest responses attributed to it in Hellenistic times are found in the usual hexameters, but our evidence from the Imperial age gives such varied rhythms as iambic trimeters and tetrameters, trochaic tetrameters and anapaestic tetrameters. This certainly suggests a new effort to enliven and diversify the utterances of the oracle.

The great outburst of activity at Claros may be fundamentally explained, as we have suggested, by the prosperity and increased population of Asia Minor. But that is only part of the story. Louis Robert has already given a preliminary survey of the cities from which the embassies came and this casts an interesting light on the clientele. Except for one entry from Corinth, there are none of the towns of the Greek mainland. Crete supplies two cities, but the embassies do not begin to occur with frequency until one looks north-west to Macedon and Thrace. The shores of the Black Sea whether European or Asiatic are well represented and also the inland towns of Asia Minor. But again the old Greek colonies are not as frequent as the new foundations. Cyme, Phocaea and particularly Chios appear, but not the others. Here, as Robert suggests, the probable explanation is that the other old-established cities had a long-standing connection with Didyma. If that temple in the second century A.D. had similarly recorded its embassies they would probably have filled the gaps left in the geographical records of Claros. In fact inscriptions of Didyma listing offerings in the second and first centuries B.C. contain the names of these missing communities.

So it would appear that in the Imperial period Claros had managed in the end to set up a rivalry to Didyma which may remind one of the struggles between Delphi and Dodona in the archaic period. Delphi which once had a strong hold on many of the cities of Asia Minor, as evidenced by the literary traditions of the sixth century or the inscriptional evidence of the third, had entirely lost its influence there, and the field had been divided between the alternative centres of Didyma and Claros. The success of the latter in particular, as we have pointed out, may have been due to its greater richness and elaboration of ceremonial. This showed itself not only in a new emphasis on lyric metres, sung responses and choral hymns, but also in the development of mysteries. The vaulted subterranean passages of the temple gave the setting for such activities, and our evidence even suggests that consultations took place at night with the additional opportunities which it gave for emotional and sensational presentation. It is probably correct to conjecture that the success of Claros in the second century A.D. was largely because it had transformed itself to fit the new spirit of the age. While Delphi remained rigidly conservative in its classical outlook, and Didyma modelled on it had not gone far to meet the trend of the times, Claros had adjusted itself to the development in religious thought.

The second century A.D. saw a new intensity in the search for divine help and a deeper consciousness of the supernatural as above and superior to the natural. This tendency which can be said to have begun at least by the time of Marcus Aurelius was to increase and develop till the official establishment of Christianity. Dodds has lately called this period 'the age of anxiety'.[15] The inscriptional records from Claros do not unfortunately tell us what the sacred embassies from the cities submitted as enquiries. Probably it was usually some general request for health and prosperity. The communities of the Roman empire had no scope for independent policies or important alternatives on which to ask the guidance of Apollo. But presumably the answers themselves, and perhaps still more the imposing ritual with which they were delivered, gave support and comfort to the cities which enquired. It is not likely that all this activity can be explained away as empty rivalry between the different civic bodies. Such rivalry did exist in the second century and at times occasioned a policy of useless emulation. But this explanation alone does not seem to fit the evidence. There was probably also a real urge to seek spiritual comfort and support.

(4) THEURGY AND THE CRITICS OF ORACLES

Besides the official oracles new possibilities of divination began to be developed in the second century. Under Marcus Aurelius a certain Julianus emerged as the founder of 'theurgy'. This consisted in the use of magic acts to achieve communication with the divine.[16] Its most important activities were either to animate statues so as to make them utter prophecies or to bring down supernatural powers and make them temporarily inhabit a human medium who could in the same way become a vehicle of prophecy. Julianus practiced these magic rites, and wrote books about them and published oracles in hexameter verse which he had elicited by this means. This became the foundation of a whole range of spiritualistic procedure which reached its fullest development in the next century and later under Porphyry, Iamblichus and others. The effect will certainly have been damaging to the popularity and effectiveness of the old established oracle-centres. It was possible henceforth for the learned to set up his own oracle and experiment in his own divine revelations. Also as theurgy was associated with the study of philosophy, it acquired a new prestige. While in the

classical ages witches and wizards were regarded as vulgar and con-
temptible, the new philosophers, many of them neo-Platonists, could
claim the highest intellectual and moral standing.

No doubt Julianus, Porphyry and Iamblichus were perfectly sincere
in pursuing these strange and equivocal rituals. But the same world in
which they worked provided a ready field for charlatans. The most
notorious of these was Alexander of Abonuteichos in Paphlagonia.[17]
He was unfortunate enough to win immortality from the satiric pen of his
contemporary, Lucian. Perhaps if we had enough other evidence about
him, our picture would not be so uniformly unfavourable. He set himself up in northern Asia Minor in the first half of the second century A.D.
as a prophet controlling his own oracle-centre. He claimed to be the
spokesman of a new manifestation of Asclepius in the form of a serpent,
named Glycon. His business was not confined to oracles of healing,
and a vast concourse of enquirers thronged the sanctuary. According
to Lucian the usual method was for enquiries to be submitted in
writing on sealed tablets. Alexander would take these and withdraw
into an inner *sanctum*, returning shortly afterwards with the tablets still
apparently sealed but with written replies appended. Lucian claims to
describe the mechanical methods by which Alexander was able to get
at the contents without leaving traces of having broken the seal.
Special clients received spoken answers, possibly by some ventriloquial
contrivance. At any rate Lucian estimated that the elaborate organisation which Alexander developed took in as much as 80,000 drachmae
a year, which as his normal fee was one drachma two obols meant over
50,000 enquirers.

It is significant that Alexander did not confine his activity to oracular
utterances. Besides recovering lost slaves, detecting thieves, and
disclosing buried treasure for private enquirers, he instituted a series
of mysteries with theatrical representations of Greek myths as adapted
to the theology of his new divinity. Here one may note his resemblance
to the practices of Claros where in the same way oracular enquiries
and initiation in the mysteries were combined. They had no doubt
both struck the taste of the times. Alexander's clientele must in effect
have taken away somewhat from the business of the old-established
oracle-centres, but he tactfully referred occasional enquirers to such
places as Claros or Branchidae. He may have thought it was in his own
best interests not to challenge the ancient Apolline oracles to a direct

confrontation. The opponents whom he attacked were the Epicureans who were in principle sceptical of all supernatural manifestations and the Christians who were beginning to come forward as critics of the practices of paganism.

Such a man as Alexander of Abonuteichos inevitably attracted the sceptical attacks of Lucian, who could at times also be ironical about the activities of the recognised oracle-centres. A much more sweeping offensive was undertaken a little earlier in the same century by the Cynic philosopher, Oenomaus of Gadara.[18] If we are to take his account in literal earnest he had been treated very naively by the prophet of Claros. He had consulted Apollo on some question concerning commerce and received the reply in trochaic verse:

'In the land of Trachis lies the fair garden of Heracles containing all things in bloom for all to pick on every day, and yet they are not diminished, but with rains continually their weight is replenished.'

This vague picture of an earthly paradise combined with the place-name Trachis, suggesting toil, seemed to promise to Oenomaus in the typically ambiguous diction of Apollo bountiful rewards for his labours. He was seriously put out, however, when he was told by someone in the crowd that he had heard exactly the same response given to one Callistratus, a merchant of Pontus. Further investigation suggested to Oenomaus that this stock reply had been issued to numbers of enquirers in all walks of life, who had all experienced the toil, but none of them had found the glorious garden. Two further enquiries which he made at the same shrine had had no better result. One of the two responses, at least as preserved in our manuscripts, is unintelligible without emendation. The other, also presumably meant to be interpreted allegorically, read:

'From a widely whirling sling a man shoots stones and slays with his throws geese, huge and fed on grass.'

On this obscure statement Oenomaus pours his ridicule. He had some justification, if, as we are apparently meant to assume, the prophet simply repeated a selection like this from a series of vaguely allegorical verses and fitted them to each enquirer almost at random. It would be possible to imagine such a procedure as this lying behind Tacitus' description of the oracle's functioning. But it is hard to believe that, if this was the best it could do, the sanctuary of the Clarian

Apollo would have received such veneration from the cities of Asia and Europe. Perhaps Oenomaus enquired before the oracle had properly achieved its second century A.D. revival: or private individuals may at times have come off poorly compared with the ambassadors sent by cities.

Anyway it is interesting to notice that Oenomaus, when he set out to incorporate his experiences in a book attacking Apolline prophecy, called *A detection of frauds*, did not otherwise deal with Claros. It would appear that, though we know of some who had written about that oracle, it had not really figured largely in Greek literature. Hence when Oenomaus wanted to convince his readers that the responses of Apollo were ridiculous and misleading, he sought for his examples in the utterances of the Pythia. These, far more than the words of the Clarian Apollo, were to be found throughout Greek literature, and Oenomaus vented his spleen on them. He showed no depth of analytical criticism, but trounced Apollo for the ambiguities which had been the conventional form of early oracular composition.

(5) PAGANISM VERSUS CHRISTIANITY

The significance and value of oracular revelation were shortly to be-come the subject of much greater debate. About A.D. 180 when Celsus produced the first comprehensive attack on Christianity from the philosophic standpoint in a book called *The True Word*, he based one of his major arguments in defence of the pagan gods on the genuineness of their oracular revelations. This threw down a challenge to the Christian apologists which they eagerly took up. Clement of Alexandria writing about the end of the century could contemptuously treat the oracle-centres as already defunct, and scornfully reject the evidence of their responses. It was no doubt true that Dodona had ceased to function and Delphi may have virtually stopped again after its temporary revival under Hadrian, but Claros was undoubtedly still in operation, though its activity may already have begun to decline and the same was true of Didyma. In the middle of the third century Origen wrote a systematic reply to Celsus, and about the same time Porphyry, as a youthful philosopher, before he had met Plotinus, produced a book on 'the Philosophy to be derived from Oracles'. This treatise was largely based on a revival of the theories of Julianus the theurge and a review of the *Chaldaean Oracles* which he had published. This movement brought the question of divine pronouncements again into the forefront of the controversy. Also the branch of the neo-Platonists led by Iamblichus devoted itself to exploring the possibilities of mediumistic prophecy.[19]

The effect of these tendencies on our literary sources is that they cease to provide information about ordinary enquiries by cities or private individuals. The texts of oracles quoted in the Christian apologists are either concerned with the decline of the prophetic centres or with the nature and identity of the deities who speak through them. Already before the time of Plutarch pagan philosophers had accepted the theory that the words of the prophets and prophetesses might be inspired, not by one of the great gods, but by a subsidiary *daemon* acting as his agent. The activities of theurgists had strengthened and extended this picture of a vast hierarchy of different supernatural powers. Also in the process they had come to accept the view that behind and above all these in majesty almost unapproachable dwelt the supreme power of which the old classical gods had been manifestations. This was a long way from the belief of the classical Greeks, and it was in many ways not very distant from the faith of the Christians.

The Christian apologists, when they wanted to refute the argument from pagan oracles, did not need to deny the authenticity of such manifestations. Epicureans and Cynics might attempt to explain them away entirely as instances of human trickery or delusion. But this interpretation would not have commended itself to the majority of contemporaries in the third and fourth centuries A.D. The sceptical viewpoint which had once appealed to many thinkers in the classical world was by that date generally abandoned in favour of a tendency to accept supernatural agencies as at work in the world. So the disagreement between Christians and pagans could turn simply on the question of the identification of the spiritual powers who operated oracles. To the pagan philosophers they were *daemones*; to the Christians they were devils, who took on the personality of Apollo as a mask to conceal their nefarious purposes in misleading mankind. The Pythia in their view was genuinely entered by a spirit, but it was an evil spirit plotting against the true God. Hence, since even devils had very special powers, the Delphic oracle might at times in its riddling ambiguities convey a correct forecast of the future, though only the better to tempt and mislead the sons of men.

The oracles quoted from Porphyry by Christian apologists are made more difficult to use as evidence by the fact that Porphyry does not appear to have troubled to indicate what oracular centre, if any, was the source of his material. He seems to have been content to attribute the responses to Apollo without distinguishing whether they were uttered at Delphi, Claros or Branchidae. Some even suggest by their content that they may simply have been extracted by a theurge from a human medium. Presumably for the purposes of Porphyry's argument any utterance of Apollo, from wherever derived, was equally valid, as a basis for logical propositions. Similarly the Christian apologists who quote these responses for mocking purposes are not interested in their local source, but are content that a pagan philosopher had used them as evidence.

Our last illustrations of oracular activity show the priesthood attempting to justify the failure of their activity. Porphyry quoted a response to the people of Nicaea (which town of the name is not explained) which ran:

'It is not possible for the spoken omen of Pytho to break forth, for already made faint by the length of time it has put on unprophetic silence. Yet offer to Phoebus as is the custom the sacrifices prescribed by the god.'[20]

One can sympathise with the wish of the priests to maintain the traditional ritual of sacrifice even when the oracle itself was defunct.

When the responses do not give such gloomy pictures, their subject, at least as preserved by our sources, is mostly theology. In the archaic and classical periods the Greeks had taken their gods for granted. The very fact that the oracle was consulted implied at least a belief in the deity's existence and, as for his precise identity, simple folk no doubt accepted vague traditional stories, and the more sophisticated, while believing that no one man really knew more about the gods than another did, accepted the ancestral ritual as binding. The third century A.D. was different. In the struggle with Christianity the pagans felt the need to assemble a body of revelation, if not exactly a creed. The era of philosophic scepticism was generally past, and the urge was felt for some syncretistic formula which would explain and combine the manifestations of religion. This could only be supplied with authority by an oracle and Macrobius, for example, quotes the following as a response given by Apollo of Claros to the question with which of the gods he who was called Iao (Jehovah) was to be identified:

'Those who have learnt unsearchable mysteries are bound to conceal them, but if you have only a tiny intelligence and a feeble mind, take note that Iao is the highest of all gods; in winter he is Hades, and Zeus in budding spring, Helios in summer, and in autumn bountiful Iao.'[21]

Here we see an attempt to combine on the basis of the seasons a supreme god in four aspects: Hades and Zeus, the sun-god (probably thought of as Apollo) and Dionysus. For Iao was sometimes explained as a title for Dionysus and at other times recognised as the name for the god of the Jews. If this is a genuine utterance of the Clarian sanctuary it shows a brave endeavour not only to combine the leading gods of paganism, but even to make room in the oecumenical system for the Jews and Christians, provided they were prepared to come in on these terms.

The antagonism between Christianity and the oracles was not to be resolved on these lines. Instead it was believed in Christian circles at least that the final impulse for their persecution under Diocletian came from oracular inspiration. The statement appears first in the contemporary treatise *On the deaths of the Persecutors* (probably by Lactantius) where the oracle of Apollo at Didyma is held responsible and the idea is repeated more vaguely in the memorial which Eusebius wrote on Constantine and his relation to the Christian Church.[22] There the emperor is even credited with an edict against oracles. Whether he actually went so far as Eusebius represents may be questioned. But generally the end of the oracle-centres came with the official establishment of Christianity, and it may have given the opportunity for particular local action then or later against the sites. At least it is significant that at Delphi the *adyton* and at Dodona the probable location of the oak-tree have shown to the modern excavator evident signs of deep disturbance. It would appear that when their opportunity came, the Christians set out systematically to extirpate what they regarded as the special home of demons.

The emperor Julian in his other activities to revive paganism attempted also to call back the oracles. The story of his unavailing enquiry at Delphi is well known. He sent a famous doctor, named Oribasius, but the answer which came back was utterly despairing.

'Tell the king, the fairwrought hall has fallen to the ground. No longer has Phoebus a hut, nor a prophetic laurel, nor a spring that speaks. The water of speech even is quenched.'

How this response had been evoked is not explained. Probably the
priest of Apollo, if the office still survived, composed this epitaph on
the Delphic oracle.

With Julian's death silence fell once more on the pagan sanctuaries,
except perhaps at Ammon. There in the recesses of the Libyan desert
it is possible that the traditional rites of consultation still persisted,
though probably they were never visited by enquirers from Europe.
At last Justinian is credited with the final act of suppression.

NOTES

1. Parke and Wormell, *Delphic Oracle*, *1*, 266 ff.
2. Livy, *22*, 57, 5 and *23*, 11. 1 ff.
3. Livy, *28*, 45, 12 and *29*, 10, 6; Magna Mater: Livy, *29*, 11, 5
4. Perseus: Livy, *41*, 22; Sulla, App. *Bellum Civile*, *1*,97; Cicero: Plutarch: *Cic.*5
5. Strabo, *17*, 1, 43
6. Praeneste: Cicero, *de Divinatione 2*, 85; Antium: Macrobius, Saturnalia, *1*,
   23, 15, Livy, *22*, 1, 11, A. Degrassi, *Inscriptiones Latinae Liberae Rei Publicae*,
   2, 289 ff.
7. Juvenal, *6*, 552. cf. Nilsson, *Geschichte der griechischen Religion*, 2, 405 ff.
8. Nero: Suetonius, *Nero*. 40
9. Plutarch, *De Defect. 3*, 411E and 414B
10. cf. p.78. supra
11. Plutarch, *De Pythiae Oraculis, 3*, 408B and 409A
12. *Certamen*, 12
13. Tacitus, *Annals*, 2, 54
14. Charles Picard, *Ephèse et Claros* (1923), now seriously out of date. L.
    Robert, *Les Fouilles de Claros*, conference donnée a l'Université d'Ankara,
    le 26 October 1953, Limoges, 1954, and preliminary reports in *Anatolian
    Studies* (1951–60)
15. E. R. Dodds, *Pagan and Christian in an age of anxiety* (1965)
16. E. R. Dodds, *The Greeks and the Irrational*, appendix II. Theurgy: pp. 283 ff.
17. Lucian, *Alexander*, passim
18. Extracts from Oenomaus occur throughout Eusebius, *Praepartio Evangelica*,
    books 5 and 6. The consultations of Claros are described in 5, 22 and 23
19. Celsus' work is reconstructed by Otto Glockner, *Kleine Texte*, no. 151,
    Bonn, 1924. Clement of Alexandria, *Protrept* 2. John J. O'Meara, *Porphyry,
    Philosophy from Oracles in Augustine*, Paris, 1959
20. Porphyry in Eusebius, *P.E. 5*, 16
21. Macrobius, *Sat.* 1, 18, 18 ff. and see Nilsson, *Geschichte der griechischen
    Religion*, 2, 457
22. Lactantius, *de morte persec.* 11, Eusebius, *Vita Constantini*, 2, 50
23. Julian: Parke and Wormell, *1*, 289 and 2, no. 476. For doubts on its authen-
    ticity, C. M. Bowra, *Hermes* (1959), pp. 426–438

CONCLUSION

An account of the ancient oracles is bound to be determined largely by the limitations of our literary sources. Literature can be supplemented from inscriptional evidence, but only to a meagre extent.[1] Excavation has yielded numerous enquiries inscribed on lead from Dodona, but no replies. Other sites have been more disappointing. Delphi among its numerous inscriptions contains very few which concern the Pythia directly. Claros preserved many records of embassies from cities, but no precise indication of their question or answer. The shrine of Trophonius once contained the tablets describing the experiences of enquirers, but all have disappeared. One can only guess what the record might have held on the analogy of the inscribed records of the medical cures at Epidaurus.

In literature the oracles figure more in the mythical than in the historical accounts. Often at the core of a legend lies a god's prophecy: that Laius will be slain by his son, that Pelias must beware of the man with one sandal, and countless other examples. Often they are attributed to Delphi, but quite probably had no original connection with that or any other sanctuary. They simply represent the mechanism by which the teller of early stories was able to put his narrative in train. Another type of unhistoric traditions about the far past consisted of aetiological legends explaining the origin of some strange cult-practice or divine title. These were sometimes complicated tales with the oracular response providing the authority at the end, but at other times we are simply told that it was custom for this or that to be done 'in accordance with a certain oracle'. Critical research can rarely hope to find any kernel of historic truth in these materials.

Of the enquiries attributed to historic periods by far the majority are presented by city-states or kings. This selection cannot correspond at all correctly to the actual business of the prophets, which must numerically have been concerned to a very large extent with the private enquirer. But our literary sources do not set out to give a well balanced picture of the typical work of an oracle. They record the episodes which are important for their specific purposes and these are often those which struck the popular imagination. Consequently the actual words reproduced came probably not from official records, but from the popular tradition about the occasion. If any Delphic records existed, no trace survives to suggest that anyone published extracts from them. Even Plutarch, though a priest of Apollo, does not appear to go back to any special sources. He reproduces a number of responses which are otherwise unknown, but there is no indication that they came from official chronicles.

One must also allow for the circumstance that many of the stories were obviously framed to glorify the god who had given the response. If it contained a prophecy this must have been fulfilled. It was, however, accepted that the gods spoke in riddles, and so the fulfilment might not correspond to the literal meaning of the utterance. In fact the more obvious the statement, the more likely (at least in the popular tradition) that it would be accomplished in some other improbable way.

Many of these stories came from the guides at Delphi who as they conducted parties round the various dedications which lined the sacred way would divert their audience with stories explaining the reason why a particular city had made this offering to Apollo. No doubt often the dedications were actually sent in gratitude for a favourable outcome to an enquiry. But also it is often probable that the story as preserved represented a ridiculous embroidery on the original facts. Even the circumstance that the guides quoted a response in verse need not be taken to show that they had preserved the historic tradition. Plutarch and his friends regarded some of these stories with complete contempt, because of their silly content and the poor literary style attributed to the god.

Other responses may have had a more dignified origin, even if actually their words were equally fictitious. For instance, though some of the early oracles for the founding of colonies may be genuine, others are apocryphal. The Pythia may have been consulted originally and may have given a favourable response, but this response either was not preserved or had no literary feature to commend it. When later someone turned out a neat piece in hexameters, his action would not be regarded as forgery any more than if he had been an ancient historian who had composed a suitably rhetorical speech to put into the mouth of a politician of the past. The foundation oracle thus framed served simply to give canonical form to the tradition that the colony had received divine sanction.

Some responses attributed to the Pythia may even have been fabricated not by the Delphic guides, but by the priests themselves. The story of Croesus' consultation is so complicated and of such high literary quality that it is not likely to have emanated from a lower level than the priesthood. But it was rare that it was necessary to compose a suitable *apologia* on a large scale for the oracle's mistake. Also in most instances no doubt if the priests had attempted to put in circulation a completely fictitious account of an enquiry, it would have been liable to be contradicted by the city authorities to whom the response was supposed to have been delivered. But the Lydian monarchy had not survived to contradict the Delphic priesthood. Unfortunate responses could more often be explained away by ingenious reinterpretation or else could be tactfully forgotten. In later times the Delphians may have chosen to forget the oracle discouraging the Cnidians from resistance to Persia, which Herodotus collected from the recipients.

With all these handicaps to the use of our tradition about oracles it is not surprising that it is difficult to sum up their policy and effect on Greek civilisation. Scarcely any individual instances are so well attested that there is no room for doubt about their historicity. Some scholars would accept one example, others another. A conclusion cannot be reached by adding up the particular instances, but only by weighing their general effect. For this purpose not enough is preserved of the responses attributed to Dodona or other oracles to justify any conjecture about their policy. Delphi alone in the archaic and classical period can sometimes be detected as following something like a consistent line on some questions. The priests seem to have encouraged the sending out of colonies, but the belief that Delphi acted as an actual clearing-house for geographical and economic information for intending colonists is probably much exaggerated. The earliest tyrants such as Cypselus were generous to Apollo and were given oracular encouragement. Later, however, the conventional picture was that the Pythia was unfavourable to tyranny. Probably this only shows how the Delphic authorities were content to let the oracle's supposed attitude correspond to popular feeling. Croesus had probably received strong encouragement and his failure had correspondingly shocked the prophets and induced in them a cautious attitude towards Persia. This led to Delphi adopting at first a very equivocal policy during Xerxes' invasion, which was only changed after Salamis.

In all this we can probably observe the typical reactions of a small Greek town whose leading citizens must have been very conscious that they had no physical resources capable of protecting the vast treasures of their sanctuary. In theory from 581 B.C. at latest they were under the guardianship of the Delphic Amphictyony, but that was a large and cumbrous body which could only act very slowly and was itself powerless against such colossal threats as the Persian invasion. So it was expedient for the Delphians to win powerful friends at all times and play for safety, as they conceived it, in international relations.

In religious and moral questions also a certain tendency can be observed. In the seventh century B.C. Delphi had encouraged the belief that murder involved ritual impurity and was properly atoned for by ceremonial purification. This tended to stress the moral aspect of the act in contrast to the more primitive emphasis on blood-feuds and blood prices. In the sixth century the moral teaching of the oracle takes clear shape with the Delphic maxims. These have in common a certain cautious restraint which may itself again express the mental attitude of the citizen of the small town. But this interpretation would limit too severely their force and application. Delphi instead taught the late archaic period that restraint and modesty which was to be the foundation on which the glorious achievement of classical art and literature was based.

One may ask how far in this Delphi was leading contemporary opinion and how far instead it was following it. The answer is probably beyond demonstration. But the most likely judgment is that while the Pythia's utterances were not in the nature of sudden apocalyptic revelations, they served to crystallise and express in memorable form the ideas of their time.

Delphi has been taken as our example in this discussion because it is the one oracle which provides a reasonable large number of instances from which to generalise. But one may conclude by stressing a different point. Though our literary traditions record almost exclusively and emphasise the highlights of the official enquiry sent by the community, the bulk of the business of Delphi was probably with private individuals and in the case of other less famous oracles it probably provided at most times their exclusive activity. Plutarch could look on such efforts with a certain faintly snobbish contempt. But while such enquirers were often ignorant and foolish, they represented a sincere attempt to find guidance in the troubles of their world. Also we need not doubt that in most instances the priests and prophetesses who gave them their answers were equally sincere in their belief that in so doing they were the agents of a supernatural power. When at times in reading the complicated explanation of some sophistically worded response to a state's enquiry we may be tempted to ask how it was that this sort of ingenuity won a great reputation for oracular wisdom, we are seeing events in wrong perspective. The high repute of the oracles rested in the end less on the claim to have achieved a few startling forecasts. It was rather the outcome of a human need. Numberless Greeks felt that they must seek a god's guidance and found it in an oracular consultation. Thus for more than a thousand years throughout the Graeco-Roman world in various places and by various means the seeker was satisfied, and the system operated till at last a new religion with new ways of access to God took its place.

NOTE

1. For a more detailed discussion of the literary evidence, see Parke and Wormell, 2, 1 ff.

BIBLIOGRAPHY

The modern study of Greek oracles begins with A. Bouché-Leclercq, *Histoire de la divination dans l'antiquité*, vols. I–IV (Paris, 1879–83, reprinted Bruxelles, 1963). It contained a very thorough survey of all the available literary evidence, but was produced before archaeology and epigraphy had made their contribution to the subject. Of more recent works there may be mentioned W. R. Halliday, *Greek Divination* (1913); M. P. Nilsson, *A history of Greek religion*, pp. 188 ff. (1925); the relevant parts of O. Kern, *Die Religion der Griechen* (1928–38); U. von Wilamowitz-Moellendorff, *Der Glaube der Hellenen* (1931–2); and M. P. Nilsson, *Geschichte der griechischen Religion* (1955); also the article on *Orakel* by K. Latte (Pauly–Wissowa, vol. 18, 1 col. 8–9 ff.) (1939) and R. Flacelière, *Greek Oracles* (1965).

On the particular oracles the following may be mentioned.

Delphi

The excavations as far as published are recorded officially in *Fouilles de Delphes* (from 1915).

On the oracle : F. Hiller von Gaertringen, Pauly–Wissowa, vol. IV, col. 2520 ff.; P. Amandry, *La mantique apollinienne à Delphes* (1950); M. Delcourt, *L'Oracle de Delphes* (1955); H. W. Parke and D. E. W. Wormell, *The Delphic Oracle* (1956).

Dodona

On the original excavations: C. Carapanos, *Dodone et ses ruines* (1878). On the recent excavations; S. I. Dakaris, 'Das Taubenorakel von Dodona und das Totenorakel von Ephyra', *Antike Kunst*, 1963, pp. 35–49. On the oracle itself: H. W. Parke, *The Oracles of Zeus* (1967)

Didyma

On the excavations: H. Knachfuss, *Didyma; die Banubeschreibung* (1939) and A. Rehm, *Die Inscriptionen* (1958). There is also a short description and discussion in George E. Bean, *Aegean Turkey*, 231–43 (1966). On the oracle: R. Haussoullier, *Revue de Philologie*, 44 (1920), 268–77.

Other miscellaneous works on oracles are: M. P. Nilsson, *Cults, Myths, Oracles and Politics in Ancient Greece* (Lund, 1951); R. Crahay, *La Littérature oraculaire chez Herodote* (1956); J. Pollard, *Seers, Shrines and Sirens* (1965).

INDEX OF PROPER NAMES